Parliamentary Pointers
for
The President
and
The Members

Alice N. Pohl

Professional Registered Parliamentarian   NAP
Certified Professional Parliamentarian   AIP

Parlie Publications

Library of Congress Catalog Card Number 85-60529
ISBN 0-918237-01-7

Library of Congress Cataloging in Publication Data

Pohl, Alice N.
   Parliamentary Pointers for the President and the Members
   1. Parliamentary practice.   I. Title.
JF515.P73   1985   060.4'2   85-12231

For additional copies
write to:
Alice N. Pohl

Parlie Publications
15525 S.W. 114th Court #31
Tigard, OR 97224-3310

ACKNOWLEDGEMENTS

To the National and International Organizations that I have served as parliamentarian and the many students and friends, I owe a debt of gratitude for their interest in correct organization procedures which stimulated the writing of this book. The questions which have been asked of me during the past years directed me in planning the form of this book and the type of material included in addition to basic parliamentary procedure.

To Floyd M. Riddick, Parliamentarian Emeritus U. S. Senate, Committee on Rules and Administration and to Frank Roberts, Senate Chamber, Oregon Legislative Assembly, Salem, Oregon, I am indebted for having reviewed the manuscript and for giving valuable suggestions.

Alice N. Pohl

INTRODUCTION

This book deals primarily with the rights and duties of the presiding officer and the members of an organization. The material in the book is based principally on Robert's Rules of Order Newly Revised, including updated procedures. It is arranged in logical order for easy reference. It is designed to present the basic knowledge in the clearest possible manner.

It is my hope that the book will meet the needs of the presiding officer and the members and help them put democratic procedures into their meetings.

CONTENTS

4
THE SECRETARY

5
MEETINGS

6
NOMINATIONS & ELECTIONS

7

MOTIONS

8

BYLAWS

1

PARLIAMENTARY PROCEDURE

101   **FUNDAMENTAL PRINCIPLES**

Parliamentary rules are founded upon principles and reason. The rules have been developed to expedite business and help the organization conduct business and carry out their aims. The object is to help and not hinder. It is not intended to confuse or obstruct. The structure of the procedure has been to make it easier for the members to work together harmoniously in expediting the business and to protect the rights of the majority, the minority and the absentee. The principles are logical and simple. Detailed technical rules should not be used for their own sake. If a person has a thorough understanding of the principles, the rules will become easier.

Every deliberative body has some rules which they have adopted, and these rules apply whenever they made a decision, or if they fail to conform to them the action becomes invalid. Every member is presumed to be equal and has rights that must be protected. If a member fails to use his rights before action is taken, he loses it.

THE PRINCIPLES WHICH GOVERN A GROUP WHEN MAKING A DECISION ARE:

1. To make a decision, the organization must meet to make that decision.

2. A proper notice of the meeting must be given to all members of the organization. Every member is entitled to such a notice of the time, place, and purpose of the meeting so that he may attend and participate.

3. There must be a quorum present at the meeting.

4. There must be a question before the body upon which it can make a decision. The question may be an oral motion or a written resolution. A member has the right to know what the question is and what its effect will be before he votes on the question.

5. There must be opportunity to debate the question. It is a member's right to hear and to be heard.

6. The question must be decided by taking a vote. The will of the majority decides. When the will of the majority has been expressed by a vote, that vote becomes the decision of the organization, except in cases where a larger vote is required. A two-thirds vote is necessary for any motion that deprives a member of his rights in any way such as: changing the rules of debate, cutting off of debate, closing nominations, closing the polls. No member can be compelled to vote. Those who do not vote when a vote is taken, silently vote with the prevailing side.

7. A decision made is null and void if it is in conflict with higher authority, such as: the constitution, bylaws or other rules of the organization, or with national, state, or local law.

8. The minority has rights which must be protected. The decision belongs to the majority, but the right to discuss, the right to be heard and the right to oppose are valued rights of a minority.

9. Only one main proposition, or subject (main motion — resolution) may be before the assembly at a time. When the main proposition is under consideration, it must be adopted or rejected by a vote, or the assembly may take other action to dispose of it by means of secondary motions before any other business can be brought up.

    Secondary motions have an order of precedence and can be made while the main motion is pending. When a secondary motion is before the assembly it becomes the immediately pending question, the main motion remains pending while the secondary motion is also pending. Secondary motions are procedural or are emergency in character. Since there are many secondary motions it is necessary to know the precedence or priority in which they must be proposed. Each motion has its rank and if the sequence is followed the proceedings will be clear.

10. A subject once voted upon, may not be presented again in the same form. The only way to bring it back for consideration in the same meeting is to move to reconsider the vote taken on the motion.

Parliamentary rules must be administered by a strictly impartial presiding officer. The presiding officer does not take part in the discussion while presiding. The presiding officer does not favor friends, but treats all members alike. Confidence in a presiding officer is attained by impartiality.

2

THE PRESIDING OFFICER

201   **THE PRESIDENT**

The most important officer in an organization is the presiding officer. The title of the presiding officer is designated in the bylaws of the organization. The word president comes from the Latin word 'praesidere' which means one who presides or is in charge of a meeting. There are other titles for the one who presides or occupies the 'chair' in a meeting. The word chair refers to the person occupying a seat of office or authority, — the one who presides over a meeting. Whatever title is given the presiding officer, that person should be addressed by that title. In this book the title 'president' will be used. While presiding, the president never uses the word 'I', but refers to himself as the 'chair'.

Presiding is an art. It is a combination of tact — sensitivity — understanding and awareness. The president should be a person having the ability to draw out ideas from the members and make them feel free and comfortable in participating in the discussion of the business. One of the causes of confusion in a meeting is the neglect of the president to keep the members informed as to what is the pending business. The position of the president is one of leadership and as the leader there are definite responsibilities and duties besides those listed in the bylaws.

1. As presiding officer, train yourself to speak-up and make yourself heard. Those sitting in the rear of the room are entitled to hear what is going on as well as those in the front of the room.

2.   Use good judgement, common sense, tact and be impartial, courteous and fair, keeping in mind that you are elected or appointed to guide the affairs of the organization, not to be a dictator or boss.

3.   The knowledge of parliamentary procedure is not given miraculously to the person when elected to office. The presiding officer needs to have some precise knowledge of parliamentary procedure to keep the meeting moving in an orderly manner and to insure equality of opportunity in decision making.

4.   As presiding officer, be a good listener. Listen to the voice of the minority, but obey the will of the majority. Be neutral when presiding.

5.   Don't depend on your 'old timers' for the answers. When planning your year, retain what is good and discard what is bad. Tradition for tradition's sake is not always good. You don't have to continue poor procedure simply because it has been done that way in the past.

6.   Study the organization's bylaws and standing rules in order to know what items to put on the agenda. Be prepared to answer any question which may arise concerning the organization.

202   THE DUTIES OF THE PRESIDENT

1.   Hold a preliminary board meeting. Present goals, or see that goals are set.

2.   Make out an agenda before the meeting by checking with the committee chairman to see if they are ready to report, and let them know the order in which you will call upon them. Check with the secretary for items of unfinished business and the order in which they should be considered. Incorporate anticipated new business on the agenda.

3.   Be sure everything is ready for the opening of the meeting.

4. Be prepared for emergencies. Be flexible. Be honest.

5. Be familiar with the bylaws and other rules of the organization, and have on hand a copy of the bylaws, standing rules, list of standing committee chairman, parliamentary authority and see that the organization is functioning under these rules.

6. Call the meeting to order at the appointed time and avoid mannerisms. Be sure a quorum is present.

7. Be non-partisan, impartial and neutral when presiding.

8. Announce, in the proper order, the business which should come before the assembly and keep things moving in an orderly manner.

9. Recognize members entitled to the floor who desire to speak or make motions.

10. State clearly all motions which have been properly proposed and restate any motion which is not clear. You may ask to have the motion in writing if it is long or complicated.

11. Make sure the members understand the pending business and explain the effect of a motion if it is not evident. Do not discuss the merits of the motion.

12. Restrict discussion to the question before the assembly. Prevent discussion getting nowhere.

13. Alternate between those speaking in favor of the motion and those speaking in opposition to the motion. Before recognizing the member ask on which side the member will speak.

14. Answer parliamentary inquiries and questions, and decide questions of order. Be courteous in giving rulings on points of order and any other question of procedure.

15. Rule improper motions out of order.

16. State the exact question to be voted upon and then put it to a vote.

17. Call for the negative vote, even though the vote seems to be all in the affirmative.

18. Clearly announce the result of each vote.

19. Expedite business, while making sure certain rights of the members are respected and protect the assembly from dilatory or frivolous motions.

20. Carry out the administrative and executive duties outlined in the bylaws or determined by the assembly.

21. Appoint a committee to approve minutes, if meetings are held less often than quarterly.

22. Enforcement of correct procedure is primarily the duty of the presiding officer, however, he cannot be expected to detect every error or omission, so this duty is shared with the members.

23. When there is no further business, adjourn the meeting. No motion is necessary.

203　POINTERS FOR THE PRESIDING OFFICER

As presiding officer you are the person responsible for the progression of the meeting. The following pointers will help you expedite the meeting and see that action takes place with due regard for the rights of everyone.

1. Begin on time, even if there are only a few present. The opening exercises or program may be conducted without a quorum present.

2. If you are not familiar with the precedence of motions have a chart of motions handy to guide you. Be familiar with the chart, or ask the advice of a parliamentarian.

3. Use the gavel to open the meeting or to call it to order. Never gavel through a motion.

4. Make sure that the members rise and are recognized by the chair before they begin to speak.

5. Call to attention those who speak without being recognized.

6. See that a motion is offered before discussion, and that it is put in the correct form — "I move that . . . ." Do not accept "I so move . . . " as a motion.

7. After a motion is made and seconded, repeat the motion and say "The motion is open to debate" or "discussion."

8. On non-controversial matters when you feel that everyone is in favor, say "If there is no objection to . . . " Wait to see if there is an objection. If there was no objection, say "Since there is no objection . . . ."

9. Be tactful to stop debate when it does not relate to the pending question. Interrupt the speaker by saying that the matter under discussion is (repeat the motion) and that the comments are not germane to it.

10. Do not let business lag. If all discussion is in the affirmative, ask if anyone wishes to speak in opposition.

11. The bylaws of the organization will usually state that the president shall appoint all standing committees with the approval of the executive committee. As soon as possible after the election make a list of suggested appointments and present it to the executive committee for their approval. Then after the committee has approved the appointments, ask the secretary to send out the following form. The form is returned to the president or secretary within a specified time.

204
SAMPLE
COMMITTEE ACCEPTANCE FORM

(Name of organization)

_____

Date

TO: _____

You have been appointed _____

(chairman) or (member)

to the committee on _____

Duties: (State bylaw provision or other)

Do you accept? _____ Yes _____ No

Please reply by _____

(date)

TO: _____

_____

_____

205
OTHER POINTERS FOR
THE PRESIDING OFFICER

1. The chair should take care that the members understand which motion is under consideration, as well as the effect of each proposed step in respect to both an affirmative and a negative result.

2. The chair should fully state the motion that is pending.

3. If the pending motion is an amendment, the chair should make it clear that it is the amendment that is being considered to be voted upon.

4. To participate in debate the presiding officer must relinquish the chair to the vice president who is present or to a ranking vice president who has not spoken on the motion and does not decline on the grounds of wishing to speak on the motion. If no vice president is in the room the president designates, with the approval of the assembly a member who has not spoken to preside. If the assembly does not approve the president's choice, nominations for a presiding officer is in order and the matter is decided by a vote.

5. The president does not relinquish the chair when the motion is made to elect officers or appoint delegates or a committee even if he is included.

6. When a member's time in debating is exhausted, the chair calls the member's attention immediately to the fact by interrupting him if necessary.

7. The president can be deposed from office for misconduct or neglect of duty by the motion to 'rescind' the election.

206   MOTIONS CONCERNING ONLY THE PRESIDENT

1. If the president is a candidate for reelection, he does not relinquish the chair.

2. If the president is nominated to be a delegate, he continues to preside.

3. If the motion is a request for resignation, or refers to the president only in a capacity not shared in common with other members, he should relinquish the chair to the vice president.

207   VOTING RIGHTS OF THE PRESIDENT

The president must instruct the assembly what to say or do in voting.

1. The president does not usually join in either the "Aye" or "No" vote.

2. In a standing or show-of-hands vote, does not participate at the first count.

3. Votes when the vote is taken by ballot.

4. *May* vote when the vote will affect the results. i.e. to cause a tie vote and defeat the motion to make or break the required 2/3 vote.

5. In a roll-call vote, votes last.

6. Cannot vote twice.

7. Is not obligated to cast the vote that will affect the result.

208   OTHER RIGHTS OF THE PRESIDENT

Holding office does not deprive the president of the rights as a member, but must be careful in exercising these rights. By virtue of the office, the president is an ex officio member of committees only if designated in the bylaws. This authority cannot be delegated to the vice-president if the president is unable to attend the regular meeting.

209   DEBATING RIGHTS OF THE PRESIDENT

1. The president as a member of the organization has the same rights, but the impartiality required of the chair precludes exercising these rights while presiding.

2.   Be neutral while presiding.

3.   To debate, the presiding officer vacates the chair and remains out of the chair until that subject being debated is disposed of.

4.   On an appeal, the presiding officer remains in the chair and may speak twice, first and last.

210   PROTOCOL FOR THE PRESIDENT

1.   Stands while:
     Calling the meeting to order
     Adjourning the meeting
     Stating the question
     Putting the question
     Explaining reasons for rulings on points of order
     Speaking on a point of order or an appeal

2.   Is seated or steps back from the lectern or microphone when the floor is assigned to a member.

3.   Avoids dwelling on technicalities as long as rights are not abused.

4.   Never uses the word "I", but refers to himself as "The Chair".

5.   The president does not leave the chair to make his report, since no action is taken on the report. The president leaves the chair if the report contains a resolution.

6.   As soon as one thing is disposed of, the president should announce the next business in order.

7.   The presiding officer has to know how to rule out incorrect procedure, frivolous and abused motions graciously and gracefully.

The presiding officer needs to know more than "how to call a meeting to order." Skill in leadership is important and this skill comes from knowing and "feeling at home" with parliamentary procedure.

211   THINGS THE PRESIDENT CANNOT DUE WHEN PRESIDING

1. The regular presiding officer knowing that he will be absent from a meeting, cannot in advance authorize another member to preside on his place.

2. Cannot ask for a second to a motion.

3. Cannot close debate so long as any member who has not exhausted his right to debate desires the floor.

4. Cannot vote twice, once as a member then again in his capacity as presiding officer.

5. Cannot be compelled to vote.

6. Cannot depart from the prescribed order of business after the agenda has been adopted. A member may move to suspend the rules to change the order of business.

7. Cannot debate while in the chair, except on an appeal.

8. Cannot "take from the table" a motion that was laid on the table.

9. Cannot conduct business by phone, except by conference phone.

10. Cannot take sides; must be impartial.

11. Does not join in on the "Aye" or "No" vote.

12. The president is not automatically an ex officio member of all committees, unless authorized by the bylaws.

13. The president cannot take a voice vote when the bylaws require a ballot vote.

14. Cannot declare a vote unanimous unless that motion was voted on by ballot and there is no negative votes.

15. Cannot impose a penalty or order an offending member from the hall.

212   THE PRESIDENT-ELECT

Some organizations elect a president one term in advance. This person is referred to as President-Elect. This office exists only if it is provided for in the bylaws. This means that members never vote for a candidate for the office of president, but would elect a president-elect and the other officers of the organization.

Once a person has been elected president-elect, the organization cannot alter the decision regarding the succession or vacate the office for other reasons.

The president-elect usually assumes the duties of the president when that officer is absent or incapacitated; however, this must be provided for in the bylaws. If this provision is not made, the first vice president would preside and complete the president's term.

A SUGGESTED FORM ON WHAT THE BYLAWS SHOULD STATE ABOUT THE PRESIDENT-ELECT:

Article 1

Officers

Section 1.   The elected officers shall be a president, a president-elect, a vice president, a . . . . etc.

Section 2.   The elected officers shall take office _____ and shall hold office for (one — two) years or until their successors take office. At the expiration of the term in such office, the president-elect shall succeed automatically to the office of the president. In the event the president-elect is unable to succeed to the office of the president, the (organization — convention) shall elect a president.

Section 4.   The office of president-elect who succeeds to the presidency due to vacancy shall be filled by a vote of the Board of Directors. The member so appointed may not succeed automatically to the office of president, but shall be eligible for election as president-elect or president if a vacancy in the office exists. Other vacancies on the Board shall be filled by a vote of the Board.

213   THE IMMEDIATE PAST PRESIDENT

A past president is one who, having been elected and has served to the end of the term, or has ceased to hold that office by reason of death before the expiration of the term.

If the bylaws of an organization state that the *immediate* past president is automatically on the board, this applies only to the person who served as president at the end of that term. It does not apply to previous past presidents.

214   EX OFFICIO

The president has such authority only insofar as the bylaws provide. In some organizations the bylaws provide that the president is an ex officio member of all committees except the nominating committee. This gives the president the same rights as the other committee members, but is not obligated to attend the meetings, nor is the president counted in determining if a quorum is present.

In some organizations, the Board includes other ex officio members. These persons are members of the board by virtue of a particular office or a committee chairmanship. An ex officio member has all the rights, responsibilities, and duties of any other member, including the right to vote.

3

THE MEMBERS

301   **THE MEMBERS**

A member of an organization has in addition to his rights as a person, associational rights. These rights are different in each organization because they are provided for in the bylaws of the organization.

The rights of each member are definite and are protected by law; they must, however, be regarded in relation to the rights of other members and the rights of the organization.

In order to assert rights, a member must choose the proper time and must follow the proper procedure.

Unless otherwise stated in the bylaws, the members are responsible for the approval of matters pertaining to the policies, program, budget and election of the officers and directors.

Since it is practically impossible to have every member present at its meetings, it is necessary to allow a certain proportion of the membership to transact the business of the organization. This proportion of the membership is called the quorum. If a majority of the membership is present and assembled in one room or area, the business can be transacted regardless of the number of members actually voting.

A quorum is the number of members entitled to vote who must be present at a meeting in order that business can be legally transacted. A quorum always refers to the number present and not to the number actually voting. The number which constitutes a quorum should be provided for in the bylaws. A quorum should be the minimum number of members who must be present to transact legally binding business.

302   THE MEMBERS — RIGHTS AND DUTIES

Parliamentary Law is built upon rights, — rights of the majority, of the minority, of the individuals, of the absentees. Every member is responsible for seeing that these rights are respected.

When a person joins an organization, he acquires certain fundamental rights. The organization may in its rules give whatever additional rights it chooses to its members.

THE INHERENT RIGHTS OF MEMBERS ARE:

1. To expect the meeting to begin on time.

2. To expect the meeting to be properly conducted.

3. To receive notices of the meetings.

4. To attend the meetings.

5. Members may be obligated to attend certain meetings.

6. To abide by the rules.

7. To respect the officers.

8. To be loyal and have faith in the organization.

9. To explain or discuss his motion.

10. To discuss a question fully and freely without interruption, subject to the rules applicable to all other members.

11. To have the question divided whenever the motion contains two or more distinct propositions, each of which is capable of standing alone and each of which may be considered and voted upon independently of the other.

12. To request information from the presiding officer.

13. To ask an explanation on any pending question which he does not understand.

14. To raise a point of order when the presiding officer does not notice a mistake or an omission.

15. Two members may appeal from the decision of the chair.

16. To nominate.

17. To be nominated.

18. To vote.

19. To abstain from voting.

20. To know the question and its effects before voting.

21. To vote for himself when he is a candidate for office.

22. To resign, if all obligations to the organization have been fulfilled.

23. To have a hearing before expulsion or other penalty.

24. To inspect official records of the organization.

25. To insist on enforcement of the rules of the organization.

26. To exercise any right given by the Constitution, Bylaws, or Rules of the organization.

27. A member cannot be assessed for any additional payment aside from dues unless it is provided for in the bylaws.

28. A member cannot be compelled to vote.

29. A member may be obligated to serve on committees.

30. A member cannot make two unrelated motions.

31. A member has no right to read from a book, etc. in debate if any other member objects.

32. A member has no right to disturb the assembly by whispering, walking across the floor, etc.

33. A member is out of order who:

> Rises or stands while another has the floor.
> Refuses to yield the floor as directed by the chair.
> Calls out after another has risen or been assigned
> the floor — a motion to adjourn
> a motion to table
> "question"

DUTIES OF THE MEMBERS

1. Be familiar with the rules and customs of the organization.

2. To carry out the obligations assigned to him.

3. To pay attention to the speaker.

4. To pay attention to business.

5. To know the basic steps in presenting a motion.

6. Confine remarks to the question before the assembly.

7. Direct all remarks to and through the presiding officer and not directly to another person.

8. Abstain from remarks outside the meeting which might in any way interfere with the work being done by an officer or committee.

9. Further the objectives of the organization.

303　　**POINTERS FOR THE MEMBERS**

Motions should be stated in the affirmative, as it would confuse members who might think they are voting for the motion when in reality they are voting in opposition. It is often possible to express a negative idea in affirmative words.

Example: "I move that we do not instruct our delegates."

This is negative wording and therefore objectionable. The maker of the motion could phrase it this way:

"I move that our delegates be uninstructed."

A member may change his unwritten vote between the time he votes and the time the chair announces the result. When the chair says: "The motion is carried" or "the motion is defeated", a member loses the chance to change his vote without the permission of the assembly.

Change of vote is acceptable in voting by show of hands, voice vote, roll call or standing vote. With a written ballot change of vote is not possible, since there is no way of showing how the member voted the first time.

To change the vote:

Example: "I ask permission to change my vote from 'Aye' to 'No' or vice versa."

Chair:　"Does any one object?"

If no one objects, permission is granted. If some one objects by calling out 'objection' the member may move that he be permitted to change his vote. The motion must be seconded and a majority in the affirmative will give the member the right to change his vote.

It is "out of order" for a member to be standing while another person has the floor, except for the purpose of making one of the following motions:

MOTIONS WHICH MAY INTERRUPT A SPEAKER

1. A point of order

2. A question of privilege

3. A point of no quorum (doubting a quorum)

4. A call for the orders of the day

If a member has been assigned the floor but has not commenced to speak the following motions may interrupt the one who has the floor:

1. An appeal from the decision of the chair

2. A parliamentary inquiry

3. A question of information

4. Giving notice of reconsideration

5. An objection to the consideration of a question

6. A motion to divide a motion

Usually the first person who rises and asks for recognition when no member has the floor is entitled to be recognized. When two or more persons rise to claim the floor, the member who rose and addressed the chair first is entitled to be recognized. When several seek recognition at the same time the following will help decide which member should be recognized.

1. Preference is given to the proposer of a motion or to the committee chairman who has presented a report. The person who made the motion is allowed to speak first to the motion. The person who made the report should be allowed to speak to the report.

2. A member who has not spoken has prior claim over one who has already discussed the question.

3. The presiding officer should alternate between proponents and opponents of a motion. The chair may inquire which viewpoint the member will present. The presiding officer can divide the opportunity to speak more equitable.

A member who remains silent when presumably aware that he has been named to a duty is regarded as accepting, and he thereby places himself under the same obligations as if he had expressly accepted.

A MEMBER IS OUT OF ORDER WHO:

1. Addresses another member instead of the chair in debate.

2. Uses the names of members in debate.

3. Fails to confine his remarks to the merits of the pending question.

4. Persists in speaking on completely irrelevant matters.

5. Makes a motion and then speaks against his motion.

6. Speaks without first having risen, addressed the chair and obtained the floor.

7. Speaks longer than permitted by the rules of the body.

8. States in debate that the other's statement "is false" but might say, "I believe there is strong evidence that the member is mistaken."

9. Disturbs the assembly by whispering, walking across the room, or in an other way.

304   HANDY PARLIAMENTARY PHRASES FOR THE MEMBERS

1. In addressing the chair:

   Mr. President — Madam President
   Mr. Chairman — Madam Chairman
   Mr. Moderator — Madam Moderator

2. I move that . . . .

3. I move to amend the motion by . . . .

4. I speak in favor of the motion . . . .

5. I speak in opposition to the motion . . . .

6. Division or I call for a division (doubt the vote)

7. Is there a quorum present?

8. I rise to a point of information.

9. I rise to a parliamentary inquiry.

10. I move to suspend the rules and take up . . . .

11. I rise to a point of order.

12. I appeal from the decision of the chair.

13. I object to the consideration of the motion (resolution).

14. Mr. President, will the member yield for a question?

4

THE SECRETARY

401   WHAT IS A SECRETARY?

There are many kinds of secretaries such as: executive, financial, corresponding, and recording. Whenever the simple term 'secretary' is used it usually means the recording secretary. In some organizations this officer is called the Clerk or Recorder. In this book we will be speaking of the recording secretary.

Secretaries usually handle a variety of details in addition to being in charge of the records, minutes of the meeting and related affairs of the organization. The secretary is an official who sits close to the presiding officer and observes carefully all the proceedings and by taking notes is able to explain at any time what business is pending. The secretary, as a member of the organization, does not forfeit any rights of membership. The secretary has the right to make motions and enter into discussion and vote, but a wise secretary knows that it is better to listen and record what is being done. Sometimes it is not expedient to exercise a right.

A good secretary is one with an understanding of the purpose of the organization and the procedures to accomplish the task; one who is able to spell correctly and to write legible minutes, letters and other records. A secretary must be able to read aloud effectively.

402 DUTIES OF THE SECRETARY

1. Prepare the Meeting Schedule.

At a meeting matters to be brought up are usually known in advance. By preparing a list of topics as an outline for the meeting can avoid confusion and wasted time and insure that everything important is covered. An order of business which incorporates the committees which are ready to report, the unfinished business from the last meeting, and any suggestions which were received should be given to the presiding officer before the agenda is typed. It may be the responsibility of the recording secretary to type and reproduce the agenda or it may be done by the presiding officer. A copy of the agenda is primarily for the presiding officer, however copies may be sent to the members or handed to each member at the meeting.

2. At the Meeting.

In the absence of the president or vice president, the secretary calls the meeting to order and presides until a chairman pro tem is elected.

3. Taking Notes.

It simplifies the taking of the minutes if information is obtained before hand. The secretary should be prepared with an outline of the items to be presented, also have a list of the members and check the names of those present or absent. Be sure to note those who arrive late and those who depart early, an important item may hinge on whether or not a certain person heard the decision. Ask to have copies of reports before the meeting so as to understand the items to be discussed.

Take complete notes of everything that is being done at the meeting, be sure they are accurate and thorough. Be constantly alert so that you can record the new topics that are introduced. These complete 'in depth' notes will help greatly in writing the minutes that will be read at the meeting. Transcribe the notes as soon as possible. The longer you wait the vaguer will be your recollection and the harder it will be to clarify any rough spots in your notes. Do not destroy the notes until after the minutes have been approved and then for a reasonable time thereafter.

Take all notes in one note book and not on pieces of paper. Number the pages to correspond with the agenda items. Be sure to record motions verbatim. If you did not hear or understand the motion, interrupt the proceedings in order to get the exact wording. Note if the discussion was long and how the vote was taken. When a committee report is given verbally, make complete notes of the report but record just a summary in the minutes.

Remember that what is done or accomplished or left unfinished at a meeting is of the utmost importance. Take notes 'in depth' but write minutes in summary.

4. Voting.

The secretary may vote on all motions and should vote by ballot; however no one is compelled to vote. The secretary *cannot* cast the ballot of the assembly. A motion to authorize the secretary to cast a unanimous ballot is out of order. The secretary may cast the elective ballot *only* if provided for in the bylaws.

5. Other Duties.

a. Send out to the membership notices of the meetings.

b. Furnish committees with whatever documents are required for the performances of their duties.

c. Conduct the general correspondence of the organization. (That is if it is not the duty of another officer.)

d. Notify officers, committee members, and delegates of their election or appointment.

e. Furnish delegates with credentials.

f. Provide paper required for voting.

g. Follow up all action after the meeting such as: notifying persons, filing reports, etc.

h.   The secretary can make mechanical changes.

i.   It is not necessary to amend the numbers of articles, sections, or other subdivisions. It is the duty of the secretary to make all such corrections where they become necessary.

j.   In voting by mail the secretary should furnish the chairman of tellers or other officials in charge of issuing the ballot a list of the names and mailing addresses on record of all persons legally entitled to vote which the secretary should certify as correct to the date as of which the ballots are to be issued.

403   **THE AGENDA**

The secretary can prepare or assist the president in preparing the agenda. The agenda is patterned after the order of business and is essential to the success of any meeting. The agenda enables members to know in advance when each type of business will be considered.

The following pattern has been established for ordinary organizations who do not have an order of business in their rules. This pattern does not include the opening ceremonies or program part, only the business part.

1.   Reading and approval of minutes.

2.   Reports of Officers, Boards, and Standing Committees.

3.   Reports of special committees.

4.   Unfinished business.

5.   New business.

6.   Announcements.

There is no standard rule for including other topics such as: roll call, payment of bills, correspondence, initiations, inductions, etc. Each organization decides for itself where it may insert these items.

If correspondence requires action by the assembly, that correspondence is read under new business and acted upon at that time.

The term "old business" should not be used as it may confuse the members concerning business that had been disposed of. Unfinished business is any business that was deferred by a motion to postpone to a definite time or any business which was incomplete when the previous meeting adjourned. The minutes of the previous meeting will show what business is incomplete.

404 THE SECRETARY'S BOOK

The secretary's book should be a good quality loose leaf binder which should contain a copy of the constitution, bylaws, standing rules, policies, procedures, a list of the current membership and a list of the committees and their members. Copies of all minutes should be kept in a consecutive order. Written reports should be attached to the minutes or placed in a file. In this way they become an important record of an organization's proceedings and a point of reference with respect to its decisions. This record book is the property of the organization.

405 FORM OF MINUTES

The form of minutes vary with different organizations. However, minutes are a formal brief summary of the proceedings of a meeting. Minutes should answer the journalistic questions: What? Where? When? Who? Why?

Minutes should be concise and should be sufficiently clear to be understood by a person not present at the meeting.

Minutes are only prima facie evidence of what transpired at a meeting, after the reading and approval of the minutes they then become the official record of the transactions of the group.

In typing minutes, capitalize and center the heading that designates the meeting, double space the text and double space between each paragraph. Use wide margins. Margin heads or paragraph heads can be used for easy reference. The lines can be numbered to make it easy for reference or for corrections. Important words may be underlined for emphasis.

406   LANGUAGE IN MINUTES

The tone of the minutes should be completely impersonal with no comment whatsoever by the secretary. Adjectives and any suggestion of bias should be avoided. Members should be referred to by their titles, if any, otherwise by their surnames.

407   CONTENT OF MINUTES

1. THE FIRST PARAGRAPH:

    a. Kind of meeting: regular, special, annual, adjourned.

    b. Name of organization.

    c. Place, date, and hour.

    d. The fact that the regular presiding officer and secretary were present or the persons who substituted for them.

    e. Attendance, by roll call, sign in, or observation. (In small meetings the names of every member present is recorded or just those who are absent.)

    f. Whether the minutes of the previous meeting were read and approved as read or mailed.

2. THE BODY OF THE MINUTES SHOULD CONTAIN A SEPARATE PARAGRAPH FOR EACH SUBJECT MATTER, SUCH AS:

    a. Treasurer's report which is read for information.

b. Bills which are approved for payment.

c. Correspondence which is read for information. (Correspondence which requires action is read under new business.)

d. Committee reports condensed or entire report attached.

3. THE BUSINESS TRANSACTIONS SHOULD CONTAIN:

a. Exact wording of each motion.

b. Name of the maker of the main motions.

c. Name of seconder is not required.
(A second merely means that the person feels that the motion is worthy of consideration and not that he is in favor of it. The seconder may vote against the motion.)

d. Omit discussion, personal views, comments.

e. How the motion was acted upon, if carried or lost or how the motion was disposed of.

f. How the vote was taken: by voice, rising, show of hands, roll call or ballot. If a counted vote, record the number of votes "for" and "against."

4. OTHER ITEMS TO RECORD

a. Names of persons appointed to committees.

b. All required previous notices.

c. Important announcements.

d. If there is a program to follow the business, include the name and subject of the speaker or participants.

e. The time of adjournment.

f. The signature of the secretary. 'Respectfully sub-
    mitted' is no longer customary.

408   READING AND APPROVAL OF MINUTES

In organizations that hold weekly or monthly meetings
the minutes of the last meeting are the first item of business.

1. To refresh your memory.

2. To inform the absentee.

3. The minutes contain the agenda.

The presiding officer calls upon the secretary to read
the minutes. The secretary rises, does not address the chair
and reads slowly and clearly. At the conclusion of the
reading, the secretary remains standing while the presiding
officer asks, "Are there any corrections?" The presiding
officer does not say "corrections, deletions, omissions" as
these are corrections. If there are no corrections, the chair
states that the minutes are approved as read. If there are
corrections, the secretary makes the correction in the margin.
If there is too much to correct the secretary draws a line
through the incorrect text and indicates in the margin that
the correction is at the end of the original minutes.

Minutes are never rewritten after they have been read
or corrected. If an error is pointed out and the error is
disputed, the secretary can refer to the notes that were
taken of that meeting or the presiding officer can take a vote
to determine whether a mistake has been made in the minutes
and to correct the mistake. After the corrections have been
completed, the presiding officer may say, "If there are no
further corrections, the minutes are approved as corrected."
Or a member may move that the minutes be approved as
corrected. After the minutes have been approved, the secretary writes the word "approved" with the date, and signs or
initials the minutes. The presiding officer may also counter-
sign the minutes.

In some organizations, the minutes are reproduced and sent shortly after the meeting to the members. This gives each member the information and the opportunity to correct any error. If the minutes are mailed to the members, corrections can be made at the next meeting in the same manner as though the minutes had been read at the meeting.

409   MINUTE APPROVING COMMITTEE

In order to save the time of reading lengthy minutes in a meeting, a committee can be appointed or elected to approve the minutes. This should be done if the organization meets less often than quarterly as the lapse of time may promote mistakes due to forgetfulness. Minutes should also be approved by a committee where there is a different representation of delegates at the next meeting. One group of delegates cannot approve the minutes of a meeting when they were not the delegates at that meeting.

A minute approving committee has the responsibility for reading, correcting and certifying the approval of the minutes.

THE PROCEDURE

At the beginning of the meeting a committee should be appointed or elected. These members then take notes of the proceedings to serve as a check on the secretary's minutes. At the close of the meeting, the secretary gives or sends a rough draft of the minutes to each committee member who examines and checks the minutes according to the notes taken. If there are no errors, the member signs and returns the minutes to the secretary within the allotted time. If there are errors, the member makes the correction before signing and returning them. When the secetary receives all signed copies the final draft is then typed. The secretary signs the minutes and adds — Approved by committee — listing the names of the committee members.

At the next meeting, the presiding officer states that the minutes have been approved by a committee. However, if a member wishes to have the minutes read, a motion can be made "to read the minutes."

410   DISPENSED MINUTES

If it is necessary to dispense with the reading of the minutes, a motion can be made to "dispense with" the reading. This motion must be seconded. It is not debatable but can be amended and requires a majority vote. To save time, if the presiding officer knows in advance that some urgent business must be attended first, the presiding officer can say, "If there is no objection, the minutes will not be read at this time." Wait. Then say, "Hearing no objection the minutes will not be read." Minutes may also be postponed to be read at any later time during the meeting while no business is pending. If the minutes were not read at the meeting, these minutes must be read at the following meeting before the reading of the later minutes.

The reading of minutes should never be dispensed with unless a provision is made for correcting them.

411   SAMPLE MINUTES

Name of Organization
Regular Meeting Minutes (date)

Wide margin
for corrections

Call to order   The regular meeting of the (name of organization) was called to order by President (name) at (time and place). The Secretary (name) announced that a quorum was present.

Minutes   The minutes of the (date) meeting were ....
                (State how they were handled.)

Treasurer's   The Treasurer reported a balance on hand
Report   of .... (date)
                Income   from................._____
                Bills in the amount of .... were paid.
                Balance on hand (date)   _____.

Bills	Bills presented for payment were: 1. 2. A motion carried to pay the bills.
Committee Reports	The following committees reported. Copy of their report is attached and made a part of these minutes. 1. Membership committee If oral report is given list the 2. Program committee important facts. 3. Recommendations are acted upon at 4. the time the report is made.
Unfinished business	The motion regarding (state the content of the motion) postponed to this meeting was discussed. The motion carried and we will ....
New business	Record exact wording of every motion, usually by whom made, and how the motion was disposed of. In an election record the votes cast.
Announce-ments	The President announced the next meeting .... Other announcements ....
Adjournment	The meeting adjourned at .... (time).

Approved_____   _____

      (date)   Recording Secretary

412   OTHER FACTS ABOUT MINUTES

1.   The minutes of regular meetings are approved by general consent.

2.   When the presiding officer asks if there are any corrections, a member can move that the minutes be approved as read. This motion must be seconded and it requires a majority vote.

3.   When the minutes are approved, the word 'approved' is written at the end and initialed by the secretary and dated. The presiding officer may also initial them.

4.   Minutes may be corrected whenever the error is noticed even if it is months or years later. These minutes are not reconsidered but are corrected by means of the motion to 'Amend Something Previously Adopted.' The motion requires recognition, a second and a two-thirds vote, or a majority vote with previous notice, or a majority vote of the entire membership. The motion can be discussed and amended.

5.   Minutes of a regular meeting are not read and approved at a special meeting.

6.   Only those present at a meeting can approve the minutes of that meeting.

7.   Minutes of meetings held quarterly or longer should be approved by a committee.

8.   When minutes are published, they are approved by a committee before they are sent out. These minutes should contain reports of committees printed exactly as submitted, showing the action taken by the assembly.

9.   Minutes of an annual meeting should not be held for action until the next annual meeting a year later. A committee should be elected or appointed to approve them.

10. Minutes of a convention are usually approved by the Board or a special committee.

11. Minutes of a board meeting are not open for inspection to a member unless the board grants permission. The Board may instruct the secretary to give a summary of the board action at a regular meeting of the organization.

12. The minutes or record of an executive session are read and acted upon only in the executive session.

13. Minutes are not kept in a small committee. The Chairman generally keeps fairly complete notes of the proceedings which include opinions expressed, information gathered, and action taken.

14. All votes taken by any other method than by voice should be recorded in the minutes of the meeting.

15. When a motion to expunge something from the minutes carries, the secretary draws a line through the words and writes in the margin these words, "ordered expunged by a vote of the assembly"; this is dated and signed by the secretary. The words should still be readable to make sure that no other words were crossed out.

16. Minutes of other meetings in addition to the last meeting that have not been read previously are read in the order of the date.

413   **COMMON MISTAKES IN THE
PREPARATION OF MINUTES**

1. Failure to show the complete wording of motions. The
    minutes might read: "Mr. A presented a resolution and
    moved its adoption. After amendment it was adopted as
    amended." A resolution is a substantive part of the
    motion and should be recorded as read by the member.

2. Failure to show precise action taken on each motion
    made. The wording should be clear as to how the
    motion was amended, or if it was referred to a certain
    committee, or postponed to the next meeting, etc..

3. Failure to record important rulings. When a point of
    order is made, the chair makes a ruling. The ruling of
    the chair must be recorded in the minutes.

4. Failure to include complete signed copies of all written
    reports which were presented. Usually such items should
    be attached as numbered exhibits and made legally a
    part of the minutes by stating that the report is attached.

5

MEETINGS

501 MEETINGS AND SESSIONS

A meeting of an assembly is a single gathering of its members in one room or area to transact business and the members do not separate unless for a short recess. A meeting may last from a few minutes to several hours.

A session is a meeting or series of meetings devoted to a single order of business, program, agenda or announced purpose. When there is more than one meeting, each succeeding meeting is a scheduled meeting to continue business at the point where it was left off at the previous meeting.

502 CONDUCTING A MEETING

The minimum number of officers necessary to conduct a meeting are the presiding officer and a secretary.

The minimum number of persons who must be present at a meeting for business to be legally transacted is the quorum of the assembly. The quorum refers to the number present and not to the number actually voting on a particular question.

There are four items essential in a meeting:

1. Call to order

2. Minutes

3. New business

4. Adjournment

There are three parts to a meeting:

1. The opening: Prayer, pledge, song, welcome, introductions, etc.

2. The business: The regular order of business should be followed but should have reasonable flexibility.

3. The closing: Announcements, program, social, etc.

AGENDA

An agenda is a list of the specific items under each division of the order of business that the presiding officer plans to present to a meeting.

PROGRAM

The program for a meeting (not social) designates the hours for taking up some or all of the business to come before a meeting. The program includes the agenda, and all the subjects that must be attended to, and the order in which they are to be considered. The program covers the entire session.

503   TYPICAL ORDER OF BUSINESS

Reading and Approval of Minutes

Reports of Officers

Reports of Boards (Cabinet, Council, Executive Committee)

Reports of Standing Committees (Those listed in the bylaws)

Reports of Special Committees (Temporary, select, ad hoc)

Special Orders (Orders that were not disposed of at the previous meeting)

Unfinished Business (Business postponed from the preceding meeting)

New Business

There is no standard rule for including other topics in the order of business such as: roll call, correspondence, initiations, etc. Each organization decides for itself where it may insert these items.

Some organizations include "good of the order" or "organization welfare" after new business. This allows for specific suggestions, constructive comments, criticism, or compliments. No motions may be proposed during this time.

The regular order of business should be followed, but should have reasonable flexibility.

The order of business for a special meeting consists only of the call to order, consideration of the items of business stated in the notice of the meeting, and adjournment.

504   SAMPLE AGENDA

For the Business Part of a Meeting

Call to Order

The presiding officer calls the meeting to order promptly at the scheduled time with one tap of the gavel.

"The meeting will come to order." or "The meeting is now in order."

Ascertain if a quorum is present.

Reading and Approval of Minutes

Unless there is a prayer, pledge to the flag, song, or roll call, the first business in order is the reading and approval of the previous meeting minutes.

"The secretary will read the minutes of the previous meeting." or "The secretary will read the minutes of the ___(date)___ meeting."

Dispensed minutes are always read and approved first.

"Are there any corrections?" (Do not add deletions, omissions, etc., as these are corrections)

"There being no corrections, the minutes are approved as read."

If any corrections have been made, "If there are no further corrections, the minutes are approved as corrected." (Corrections are handled by general consent.)

If the minutes have been printed and mailed to each member before the meeting, they are not usually read in the meeting.

"The minutes have been mailed; are there any corrections to these minutes?" "Hearing none, the minutes are approved as mailed."

If the organization has a committee to correct and approve the minutes, the chair announces the fact.

Reports of Officers

At the annual meeting the officers report in the order in which they are listed in the bylaws. Usually in regular meetings the presiding officer calls on the treasurer to report. The treasurer reports the income and expenses since the last meeting. The presiding officer asks, "Are there any questions?" The questions are answered by the treasurer.

The presiding officer states, "This report was read for your information and will be placed on file." No vote is taken on the treasurer's report.

Reports of Committees

The report of the board of directors or governing body is given first. The minutes of the board of directors are not read, only a summary is given. If the board presents a recommendation, it is considered and voted upon at this time. No second from the assembly is required.

Only those standing committees who have a report to give should be called upon. The report should be worded in the third person. No action is taken on a report which contains information only.

No vote should be taken on the report of the nominating committee.

Reports of Special Committees

The special committees that are to report are called on in the order in which they were appointed.

Special Orders

Items of business that have been made special orders are taken in the order in which they were made.

Unfinished Business and General Orders

The expression "old business" should be avoided. A general order is any question which, usually by postponement, has been made an order of the day without being made a special order. "Unfinished business" is a question that was pending when the previous meeting adjourned. Or any question that was unfinished at the previous meeting. Or matters postponed to be taken up in the order in which they were made.

The chair should not ask for "unfinished business." He should have a list of all such subjects.

An item that was "laid on the table" may be taken from the table at this time or under new business.

New Business

Correspondence which require action may be brought up at this time. Members may introduce new items of business.

Announcements

The chair may make, or call upon another officer or member to make any necessary announcements.

The chair adjourns the meeting, no motion is necessary.

Any particular item of business can be taken up out of its proper order by adopting a motion to suspend the rules by a two-thirds vote. This also may be done by general consent.

505   QUORUM

Since it is practically impossible to have every member present at its meeting, it is necessary to allow a certain proportion of the membership to transact the business of the organization. This proportion of the membership is called the quorum. If a majority of the membership is present and assembled in one room or area, business can be transacted, regardless of the number of members actually voting.

While it is a members obligation to vote, no one can be compelled to vote. Those who abstain from voting accept quietly without protest the action of those who voted, otherwise if they do not agree with the majority, they have the privilege to express their views by voting.

A quorum is the number of members entitled to vote who must be present at a meeting in order that business can be legally transacted. A quorum always refers to the number present and not to the number actually voting.

The number which constitutes a quorum is usually stated in the constitution or bylaws of the organization. The quorum should be as large a number of members as can be reasonably be depended on to be present at any meeting. In the absence of a provision which constitutes a quorum, common parliamentary law fixes the quorum at a majority of the total membership of the organization. The requirement of a quorum is a protection against the unrepresentative action by a small number of persons in an organization. It is legal and common practice to fix the quorum at less than a majority of the membership. When the provision for a quorum is a small proportion of the total membership, rigid requirements for notices of meetings should be made in order that all the members will have an opportunity to be present.

Depending on the organization where there is no provision for a quorum, in accordance with common parliamentary law the quorum is:

1. In a mass meeting the quorum is simply those present.

2. In ordinary organizations with an enrolled membership whose bylaws do not specify a quorum, the quorum is a majority of all the members.

3. In a conference or convention in which there are delegates unless provided otherwise, the quorum is a majority of qualified delegates who have been registered as attending, irrespective of whether some may have departed.

4. In churches or some other organizations in which there is no required dues, and the membership list is not reliable as to the members in good standing, the quorum at a meeting consists of those who attend.

5. In committees or boards, the quorum is a majority of the members on the committee or board, unless a different

quorum is specified in the bylaws or rules of the organization. A committee or board does not have the power to determine its quorum, unless the bylaws authorize it.

PROCEEDINGS IN THE ABSENCE OF A QUORUM:

If the organization's rules require that a meeting be held, the absence of a quorum does not prevent the calling of the meeting to order. The minutes must show that the rules were complied with and the meeting was held. The only action that can legally be transacted in the absence of a quorum is:

1. To fix the time to which to adjourn.

2. To adjourn.

3. To take a recess to take measures to obtain a quorum.

Business cannot be transacted in the absence of a quorum. However, emergency action can be taken and confirmed or approved at the next meeting. The motion to 'RATIFY' (approve or confirm) is an incidental main motion that is used to make valid an action already taken that cannot become legally valid until approved by the assembly with a quorum present.

While business cannot be legally transacted in the absence of a quorum, a quorum is not required in certain situations such as:

1. Committee reports can be received for information but no action taken on them.

2. The "program of the day" can be given. In some cases a quorum may have arrived at the conclusion of the program.

When the chair called the meeting to order and a quorum was present, it is presumed that a quorum continued to be present. The fact that a quorum was actually present at any time can be established by counting the members present or by entering on the roll the names of those present regardless of whether they voted.

When a member notices the absence of a quorum, he can "make a point of order" to the effect at any time so long as he does not interrupt a person who is speaking. When the chair notices the absence of a quorum, he can entertain a motion to "adjourn" or "to fix the time to which to adjourn" or to "take a recess" to contact members and ask them to attend. In organizations that have the power to compel members to attend a "call of the house" can be ordered.

The quorum for all meetings should be established in a section of the bylaws. In changing the bylaw provision care should be taken in how it is done. An amendment to the bylaws goes into effect immediately upon its adoption, so if the number is struck out the quorum will instantly become a majority of the membership. The proper procedure to amend that part of the bylaws is to "strike out" the old provision and "insert" the new provision. This should be made as one motion and voted upon as one motion. The notice of the bylaw amendment should be formally worded such as: "I move to amend Article _____ Section _____ by striking out _____ and inserting _____ after the words ' _____ .' "

506   HANDLING A MOTION

A motion is a formal statement of a proposal for consideration by the assembly. The essential steps by which a motion is brought before the assembly are:

1. A member rises and addresses the chair and waits for recognition.

2. The chair recognizes the member.

3. The member proposes the motion by saying, "I move that . . . ."

4. Another member without rising or addressing the chair seconds the motion.

A second merely implies that the seconder wishes the motion to be considered by the assembly, but not that he favors the motion. He may wish to speak against the motion and vote against it.

A motion made by direction of a board or committee requires no second.

If a motion is not seconded, it is not before the assembly. It does not die; the chair just proceeds to the next item of business.

5. The chair states the motion, which then becomes the question. "It is moved and seconded that . . ., is there any discussion." If the wording is not clear or requires smoothing, the chair should put it into suitable form. The wording in the minutes should be the same as was stated by the chair.

6. Discussion: Speakers must

    1. Be entitled to the floor.

    2. Address their remarks to the chair; be courteous, avoid speaking about personalities.

    3. Confine the discussion to the pending question. If secondary motions are made, they become the pending question.

    4. Observe the rules as to the number of times and length of time a speaker may speak to a question.

    5. Asking for information is not counted as debate.

7. The chair puts the question by saying "Those in favor of the motion that . . . (repeat the motion or have the secretary read the motion say, 'Aye' (pronounced 'I'). Those opposed say 'No' " The chair must always call for the negative vote and tell the assembly what to say. If the chair is in doubt, a rising vote or a show of hands may be taken.

8. The chair must announce the vote. "The ayes have it and the motion is carried" or "The noes have it and the motion is lost." If the vote is tied, the motion is lost as it is not a majority. The chair may, but is not compelled to, vote to make or break a tie vote. The chair does not vote on a voice vote, in a rising vote or a show of hands. The chair always votes when the vote is taken by ballot.

POINTS FOR THE CHAIR TO KEEP IN MIND:

The correct phrase to use in making a motion is:
"I move that . . . . ."

It is incorrect to say:
"I so move"
"I would like to make a motion"
"I make a motion"

The chair may help or assist the member in stating his motion.

Important or complex motions should be put in writing.

The wording would then be, "I move the adoption of the following resolution. . . . "

IT IS THE DUTY OF THE CHAIR WHEN PUTTING THE MOTION TO VOTE:

1. To repeat the member's motion accurately just before the vote is to be taken.

2. To put it to vote clearly and audibly.

3. To announce the result correctly and distinctly.

EXAMPLE:

Chair, "There being no further discussion, the chair will put
        the motion to vote;"

1. "The question is on the motion that . . . . "

2. "Those in favor of the motion say 'Aye' " pause "Those
   opposed to the motion say 'No'."

3. "The 'ayes' have it and the motion is carried" or "The
   'noes' have it and the motion is lost."

**507   ASSUMED MOTIONS and
             GENERAL CONSENT**

One of the duties of the presiding officer is to expedite
business in every way compatable with the rights of the
members.   The chair may sometimes expedite business
matters by assuming the motion — that is — stating the
question without waiting for a formal motion by a member.

EXAMPLE:

Chair, "The minutes are approved as read (or corrected)."

Chair, (After the audit report has been read) "The question
        is on the adoption of the auditor's report. Is there
        any discussion?"

GENERAL CONSENT

In cases where there seems to be no objection in routine
business or on questions of little importance, time can often
be saved by the procedure of general consent or as it is also
called unanimous consent.

To obtain general consent, the chair states, "If there is
no objection" or "Is there any objection to . . . . ?" pause
"Hearing no objection we will . . . . "

If anyone calls out "objection" the chair states the question and takes the vote to determine the result.

Unanimous consent doesn't necessarily imply that every member is in favor of the proposed action; it only means that the opposition feeling that it is useless to oppose or discuss the matter simply acquiesces.

EXAMPLE: If a speaker's time in debate has expired and he asks for additional time, the chair may say, "If there is no objection the members time will be extended."

Amendments are sometimes so simple or acceptable that they may be adopted by general consent.

Chair, "If there is no objection the words . . . . will be inserted (or added), the wording of the motion then will be . . . ."

508   HANDY PARLIAMENTARY PHRASES
FOR THE PRESIDING OFFICER

The meeting will please come to order.

The Secretary will read the minutes of the _____ meeting.

We will now hear the Treasurer's report.

Are there any questions concerning the report of the Treasurer?

The first business in order is . . . .

The next business in order is . . . .

New business is now in order.

The Chair recognizes . . . .

It is moved and seconded that . . . .

It is moved and seconded to amend the motion by . . . .

The motion is not in order at this time.

Please repeat your motion.

Those in favor of the motion . . . . please say "Aye". (pronounced I)

Those opposed to the motion say "No".

The "Ayes" have it; the motion is carried.

The "Ayes" have it, the amendment is carried. Is there further discussion on the motion as amended?

If there is no objection the Chair will . . . .

For what reason does the member rise?

Hearing no second, the motion is not before you at this time.

If there is no further business, the meeting is adjourned.

6

NOMINATIONS & ELECTIONS

601 SELECTION OF A NOMINATING COMMITTEE

The selection of a nominating committee is extremely important as they are the ones that place in nomination the leaders of the organization. Usually the bylaws of an organization will state if the nominating committee is to be elected or appointed. It is preferable that the committee be elected. The committee may be a standing committee elected in advance to observe the capabilities of the members for the offices to be filled in the future, or it may be a special committee elected in advance of the election. The president should have no part in the selection of the committee, nor be an ex-officio member of it. Only members in good standing should be selected to serve on the nominating committee and they should represent the various interest groups in the organization.

602 THE NOMINATING COMMITTEE MEMBERS

The nominating committee members should be familiar with the membership and the organization bylaws which describe the nominating procedures. By studying the needs of the organization the committee can prepare a list of officers who can work together harmoniously as well as represent different groups within the organization. The well being of the organization should be kept in mind when considering a possible nominee. Questions such as these may be asked in the committee meeting:

1. Does the person being considered believe in the objectives of the organization?

2. Does the person have the time to devote to the duties of the office?

3. Does the person have a good relationship with others in the organization, or does he have too many cronies?

4. What has been the past performance of the person?

Members of the organization can suggest names of prospective nominees which the committee should carefully review. The nominating committee, at the first meeting should receive from the secretary a current membership list and an attendance record. The committee may meet several times in order to discuss possible candidates by reviewing their past performances and record of attendance. This information should be kept within the committee. Selection of the candidate should be by majority vote. When the committee agrees upon a prospective candidate, the candidate should be contacted while the committee is still in session to make sure he will serve if nominated and elected. The committee must have the candidate's agreement to serve if elected before the name is included in the report. Some organizations require this agreement to be signed on a form furnished by the committee. A member of the nominating committee may be considered as a candidate and it is not necessary for the member to resign from the committee if the person meets the qualifications and is willing to serve if nominated and elected. No prospective candidate should be contacted by an individual committee member prior to the committee meeting.

The number of nominees for each office depends upon the bylaws of the organization. Unless the bylaws state otherwise, the committee is not required to submit more than one candidate for each office to be filled.

After a majority of the committee has agreed upon the nominees, a report is made and signed by all members who agree to it. At the business meeting, the presiding officer asks the committee to report. The chairman of the committee usually reads the report and hands it to the presiding officer or the secretary who files the report. This report is never accepted or adopted. After the report has been read, the committee is automatically discharged, but can be revived if necessary, should a nominee withdraw before the election.

603 NOMINATIONS
Points to Remember

1. A nomination is a proposal that a certain position is filled.

2. A nomination is not an election. It is an assurance that the nominee will serve in the specified office if elected.

3. One who seeks an office is a candidate. When the candidate's name is put up for nomination, he is then a nominee.

4. The method of nominating and electing officers should be specified in the bylaws of the organization.

5. If no method is prescribed in the bylaws, a member may move that nominations be made by: (a) the chair; (b) a committee; (c) from the floor; (d) by ballot.

6. A nomination does not require a second.

7. The chair repeats each nomination until all nominations for that office has been made.

8. The same person can be nominated for more than one office. If elected to more than one office, the person decides which office. If the person is absent, the assembly decides. (A person can hold only one elective office.)

9. Nominations are usually allowed from the floor (also called open nominations).

10. No motion is necessary to close nominations. The chair declares that the nominations are closed.

11. If a motion is made to close nominations, the motion requires a *2/3 vote.*

12. Nominations may be reopened by a *majority* vote.

13. If a person is nominated and unable or unwilling to serve, he should decline immediately.

14. A nominating committee is not required to nominate more than one candidate for each office, unless the bylaws state otherwise.

15. Members may submit names to the nominating committee.

16. The nominating committee contacts each person whom it wishes to nominate and obtains the acceptance of the nomination.

17. When the report is formally presented to the organization, the committee is automatically discharged.

18. No vote is taken on the report. (The chair thanks the committee.)

19. If a nominee withdraws before the election, the committee is revived to nominate another for the vacant position.

20. If the nominee is elected and resigns, then the vacancy is filled by the prescribed method in the bylaws.

OTHER POINTS TO REMEMBER

A nomination is DECLINED (Properly speaking) after a person is elected, he may resign. (not decline)

A member cannot nominate more than one person for a given office until all have had an opportunity to nominate.

Nominations cannot be amended, — seldom debated — however, a nominating speech can be given.

Qualifications of each prospective nominee should be examined and discussed in the committee BEFORE the member is asked to become a nominee.

The committee must keep all discussion in confidence, weigh qualifications, and responsibilities, then correlate the person and the office.

The president of the organization should not appoint the nominating committee, nor be a member of it.

When only one nominee is put up and the bylaws of the organization do not require a ballot vote, the chair may take a voice vote, or the chair may declare that the nominee is elected.

604 HOW THE CHAIR HANDLES NOMINATIONS

A nomination is practically a motion that the person nominated be chosen for the position. A nomination differs from the ordinary motion in that it does not require a second nor can it be amended.

Nominations can be made 1) by the chair; 2) from the floor; 3) by a committee; 4) by ballot; and 5) by mail.

When the chair calls for nominations from the floor, a member need not rise and be recognized by the chair. However, in a large meeting or a convention the member should rise when making a nomination.

Member: "I nominate member A."

Chair: "Member A is nominated. Are there any further nominations?"

The chair repeats each nomination in this way until all nominations have been made. When it appears that no one else wishes to make a nomination, the chair closes nominations.

Chair: "Are there further nominations? If not, nominations are closed."

If a member moves to closes nominations the procedure is:

Member: "I move to close nominations."

Another member: "Second the motion."

Chair: "It is moved and seconded to close nominations. Those in favor of closing nominations, stand." "Those opposed to closing nominations, stand." "There being two-thirds in the affirmative, the motion is carried. Nominations are closed."

It takes a two-thirds vote to close nominations. This procedure takes time. The chair may say after the motion is made: "If there is no objection, nominations are closed." Pause — "Hearing no objection, nominations are closed."

In an election of officers, nominations are usually made by a committee. When the nominating committee is called upon to report, the reporting member presents the following report: "Mr./Madam President the nominating committee submits the following: for President, member A; for Vice-President, member B; for Secretary, member C; (and so on for each office to be filled naming the nominees in the order in which they are listed in the bylaws.)

The reporting member then hands the report to the president. The committee is automatically discharged. No vote is taken on the report.

Chair: "The nominating committee has nominated member A for the office of President; are there further nominations for President?"

When it appears that no one else wishes to make a nomination the chair may ask again if there are any further nominations, and if there is no response, the chair closes nominations for that office, without waiting for a motion. After nominations have been closed, voting for that office takes place, or nominations for the next office can be called for by the chair.

If a candidate is unopposed and the bylaws do not require the election to be by ballot the chair says: "Those in favor of member A for President say 'Aye'." Pause "Those opposed say 'No'. The 'Aye's have it and member A is elected President."

If the nominating committee has prepared a ballot containing the names of the nominees and space for nominations from the floor or a write-in candidate, the ballot is given to each voting member. The chair must instruct the members how to mark the ballot and how to fold the ballot.

When the balloting is completed the chair directs the tellers' to collect the ballots. In collecting the ballots it is the tellers responsibility to see that no member votes more than once. Ballots are never passed to the center isle. In a meeting where only voters are present, members can remain in their seats and drop their ballot into a receptacle passed by a teller and checked by another teller. Or they can go to a central ballot box in charge of two tellers and deposit their ballot. Or they can hand their ballot to a teller — who judges by the feel of the paper that only one ballot is being cast. The teller then deposits the ballots in a central box. Balloting should not be subject to haphazard variations from occasion to occasion.

It is out of order to move that one person — the secretary cast the ballot for the assembly.

PROCEDURE FOR PRESENTING NOMINATIONS
605   BY THE NOMINATING COMMITTEE

When a nominating committee is called upon to report, the chairman presents the report as follows:

The nominating committee submits the following nominees for office for the year (year or term of office) .

For President _____

For Vice President _____

And so on for each office to be filled.

The report is signed by all members of the committee, the chairman signing first. After reading the report, the chairman gives the report to the presiding officer.

The presiding officer says, "Thank you for this report." No vote is taken on the report. The nominating committee is automatically discharged when the report is given to the assembly.

606   PROCEDURE FOR NOMINATIONS FROM THE FLOOR

The presiding officer states "Nominations are in order for the office of President."

Member: Rises, does not need to be recognized by the chair, and says, "I nominate _____."

The presiding officer states: "_____ has been nominated. Are there further nominations?"

The chair repeats each nomination in this way until all nominations for the office have been made. When no one else wishes to make a nomination the chair declares the nominations closed for that office. A motion to close nominations is not necessary and should not generally be moved. If a member moves to close nominations, the motion would require recognition, a second and a two-thirds vote. A two-thirds vote is taken by rising.

607   PROCEDURE FOR RE-OPENING NOMINATIONS

Member: Rises, addresses the chair and waits for recognition, then says, "I move that nominations be re-opened for the office of _____ ."

Another Member: Without rising, "I second the motion."

Chair: "It has been moved and seconded that nominations be re-opened for the office of _____ ."

(This motion is not debatable but may be amended.)

Chair: "Those in favor of re-opening nominations for the office of ＿＿＿＿＿ say AYE." Pause.

"Those opposed to re-opening nominations for the office of ＿＿＿＿＿ say NO." Pause.

A majority in the affirmative re-opens nominations. If the vote is in the affirmative, the chair calls for further nominations.

608   **ELECTIONS**

1. Each organization should adopt the method of electing officers that is best suited to its own case.

2. If the bylaws require certain formalities they must be observed.

3. If the bylaws require the election to be by ballot, a motion to dispense with the ballot is illegal.

4. The secretary may be instructed to cast the elective ballot ONLY if provided for in the bylaws.

5. Where only one candidate is nominated, some method of speeding up the election should be included in the bylaws.

6. A majority vote is required to elect.

7. A plurality vote (largest number of votes cast) never elects, unless provided for in the bylaws or by a specially adopted rule.

8. An election to an office becomes final immediately, if the candidate is present and does not decline.

9. If the candidate is absent and has not consented to his nomination, the election becomes final when he is notified of his election and he does not decline.

10. A candidate can decline an election.

609   **TELLERS**

The chair appoints tellers to distribute, collect, and count the ballots, and to report the vote.

The number of tellers depends on the number of voters. (At least two or three)

Tellers are chosen for accuracy and dependability. They should not be personally involved in the election.

Ballots are never passed to the center aisle. It is the Tellers' responsibility to see that no member votes more than once.

Ballots may be handed to the teller, may be dropped into a receptacle passed by a teller, or may be deposited in a box.

The chair closes the polls when everyone appears to have voted.

610   **PROCEDURE FOR COMMITTEE**
                         OF TELLERS

1. Distribute ballots to those entitled to vote.

2. After the President declares the voting closed, collect the ballots in containers provided for that purpose.

3. Retire, preferably to another room, to count the ballots. No one else is permitted to be present.

4. Open the ballot-box and count the ballots. The ballots should equal or be less than the number of eligible voters.

5. Tally sheets should be prepared by the tellers as soon as the nominations were made.

6. If there are four tellers, teller #1 opens the ballot and glances at it; teller #2 reads the ballot aloud; teller #3 marks his tally sheet as the name is read, teller #4 also marks his tally sheet as the name is read.

7. Marking the tally sheet:

    The marks are vertical lines in groups of four with the fifth mark going diagonally across these four lines. When the teller marks this fifth line, the teller calls out "Tally." Teller #3 and #4 should be in agreement. If they do not agree, the teller who called out the name can easily recheck the last five ballots.

8. Blank ballots are not counted.

9. Misspelled words or names are counted if the meaning is clear.

10. Illegal votes are recorded.

11. The tally sheets are sealed in an envelope and retained until such time as there is no possibility of them being required, then they are destroyed.

12. The final tellers' report is compiled in duplicate.

13. The tellers return to the assembly. The chairman reads the report, giving a copy to the President to read. The *President* announces who is elected.

14. The tellers are honor-bound not to divulge the vote of anyone whose ballot they recognize by handwriting or otherwise.

611 **TELLERS REPORT**

1. The number eligible to vote _____ .

2. The number of votes cast _____ .

3. The number of votes necessary to elect _____ .

4. The number of votes received by each candidate.

   _____ received _____ votes.
   _____ received _____ votes.
   _____ received _____ votes.
   _____ received _____ votes.

5. Illegal votes _____ .

TELLERS REPORT ON A MOTION

1. Number eligible to vote _____ .

2. Number necessary for adoption Majority — 2/3 — 3/4

3. Votes for the motion _____ .

4. Votes against the motion _____ .

5. Illegal votes _____ .

A motion to make a ballot vote that was not unanimous as an unanimous vote is out of order.

One vote may be a majority. A single affirmative vote, when there is no other votes cast has been held by the courts to carry a question on the principle that it is a majority of the votes cast.

7

MOTIONS

KINDS OF MOTIONS

The transaction of business in a meeting consists of motions. An individual member makes a proposition which is accepted or rejected. This may be simple, but the members of an assembly may wish to consider the subject at a future time, or they may be willing to accept it with certain modifications.

There are two kinds of motions: PRIMARY and SECONDARY. The primary motion is the MAIN motion — the proposal or the proposition. If the main motion is accepted, it commits the assembly to do something, or to take some action or attitude. The main motion has implications beyond the conduct of this present meeting when it was proposed.

To distinguish between motions, they are classified as follows:

1. Main motions
    a.   Original main motion
    b.   Incidental main motion

2. Secondary motions
    a.   Subsidiary
    b.   Privileged
    c.   Incidental motions

3. Unclassified motions
   a. Motions that bring a question again before the assembly:
      1. Amend something previously adopted
      2. Discharge a committee
      3. Rescind
      4. Reconsider
      5. Take from the table

The difference between the original main motion and the incidental main motion is: the original main motion brings before the assembly a new substantive subject. The incidental main motion brings before the assembly some previous subject or present action to be taken up by the assembly, or some future action. Incidental main motions are treated exactly like the main motion, except that the motion to "object to the consideration" cannot be applied to it. The incidental main motion should not be confused with the secondary motions which are called "incidental motions".

A secondary motion is a procedural motion which can be made and considered while the main motion is on the floor. When a secondary motion is made it becomes the immediately pending question while the main motion remains pending. Secondary motions have priority and certain secondary motions take priority over others, so it is possible to have more than one secondary motion pending at the same time that the main motion is pending.

A resolution is a main motion and handled like a main motion. The difference between a main motion and a resolution is: A main motion is proposed by the words "I move that . . . . " A resolution is proposed by the word "Resolved, That . . . . " A resolution may have a preamble which in reality is debate before the motion is stated. A resolution presented by a committee or a board does not require a second, but all other rules pertaining to a main motion apply. The form for presenting a resolution is "I move the adoption of the following resolution, Resolved, That . . . . "

The long-form resolution consists of a preamble which begins with the word "whereas." Each "whereas" clause introduces the reasons in a logical order. The preamble attempts to include reasons for the motions adoption, however, it should include only those clauses that are necessary without which the merits of the resolution would be poorly understood or where unusual importance is attached to making certain reasons for action necessary.

702   THE PRINCIPLE OF THE PRECEDENCE OF MOTIONS

Before a subject can be considered in a deliberative assembly, it must be brought before the assembly in the form of a motion or a proposition. Only one main motion can be considered at a time. After the main motion has been stated by the chair, it is before the assembly and must be adopted or rejected or the assembly must take some other action to dispose of the motion in some way before any other subject can be brought up. A new subject cannot be introduced while another main motion is pending. However, there is a motion designed to virtually meet every situation that may arise in a meeting. The consideration of a main motion can involve a number of secondary motions. These secondary motions have been proven by their usage to enable an assembly to arrive at the general will of the members on a number of questions.

The secondary motions are classified as: Subsidiary, Privileges and incidental.

A secondary motion can be made and considered while a main motion is pending without violating the rule that only one motion at a time can be considered. Secondary motions are made and seconded and stated by the chair in the same manner as the main motion. The secondary motion then becomes the immediately pending question and the main motion remains pending. While secondary motions supersede the main motion for the time being, they also take precedence over certain other motions, so it is possible to have more than one secondary motion pending at the same time. Secondary motions have value or rank, they follow a pattern and each has its place.

It is important to know the precedence of motions. The rank of motions is fully supported by reason and logic. It is the presiding officer's duty to recognize a secondary motion, its purpose and its rank.

703   THE MAIN MOTION

A main motion is a proposal, an idea that brings business before the assembly. The proposal is made by a member that something be done or that a certain statement express the sense, opinion, or wish of the assembly.

RULES GOVERNING THE MOTION:

1. Is not in order when another has the floor

2. Requires recognition

3. Requires a second

4. Is debatable

5. Is amendable

6. Yields to any subsidiary, privileged or applicable incidental motion

7. Requires a majority vote: Except when the bylaws require a greater vote, or when adoption would have effect of suspending a rule of order or a parliamentary right, or when adopted would have the effect of rescinding or amending something previously adopted.

8. May be reconsidered

Motions that can be made while the main motion is pending are: all subsidiary, all privileged, applicable incidental motions such as: division of the question; consider seriatim, withdraw; and object to the consideration to an original main motion.

THERE ARE TWO KINDS OF MAIN MOTIONS:

1. The ORIGINAL MAIN MOTION that introduces a new subject to the assembly for consideration and action. A member may object to the consideration of the original main motion. The original main motion may be required to be in writing.

2. The incidental main motion is a main motion that is incidental to or relates to the business of the assembly or to its past or future action. It is usually made orally.

Examples of incidental main motions are:

To ratify emergency action taken at a meeting when no quorum was present.

To rescind some action or rule already adopted.

To adopt a recommendation which an officer or committee has been directed to make.

To take from the table.

To amend something previously adopted.

To reconsider.

To reconsider and enter in the minutes.

To expunge.

To limit or extend the speeches at a meeting.

A member may object to the consideration of an original main motion, but it is not in order to object to the consideration to an incidental main motion.

As a general rule a main motion should be stated in the affirmative. A motion stated in the negative is confusing to the voter. A motion should be clear and definite, it should have one reasonable interpretation and be as brief as possible. A long or complicated motion should be submitted in writing.

The form is:

"I move that . . . . "

The phrases, "I would like to make a motion" or "I make a motion" or "I so move" are not correct.

704   THE RESOLUTION

A resolution is a formally written motion. Main motions that express sentiments or are a formal statement of the opinions of the assembly are usually stated in the form of resolutions.

Introductory clauses are not always necessary to introduce a resolution. However, when special circumstances make it desirable to include a brief statement giving the background or reasons for the motion, the introduction statements begin with a "whereas" clause. The "whereas" clauses are the preamble to the resolution.

The preamble generally should contain only the clauses that are strictly necessary, such as, little-known information without which the merit of the resolution are likely to be poorly understood, or items of unusual importance.

The form of a simple resolution begins with "Resolved, That . . . . " A resolution can consist of more than one resolving clauses. Example: Resolved, That . . . ; and
Resolved, That . . . .

The form of a resolution with a preamble may be:

Whereas, A . . . . ; and

Whereas, The . . . . ; and

Whereas, The . . . . ; be it

Resolved, That . . .(stating action to be taken) . . .; and

Resolved, That . . . (stating further action to be taken). .; and

Resolved, That . . . (still further action to be taken).

In the preamble the word "whereas" introduces each item, it is followed by a comma, and the next word begins with a capital letter, and the phrase ends with a semicolon; followed by the word "and". The last "whereas" closes with a semicolon; followed by the words "therefore be it" or "be it.". These words are placed at the end of the preamble and should not be placed at the beginning of the resolving clause.

Example: Whereas, The . . . . . . ; therefore be it

Resolved, That . . . .

To introduce a resolution the member says, "I move the adoption of the following resolution, resolved . . . . . " or "By direction of the board or committee, I move the adoption of the following resolution. . . . . . "

The resolving clauses are voted on separately, as each is a primary motion. Each one is debatable, amendable, may be referred, postponed, laid on the table and debate limited or extended or closed. After the resolving clauses have been voted upon, the preamble is then put to a vote. Depending on the disposition of the resolving clauses, the preamble may be amended. The motion to stop debate on the resolving clauses does not apply to the preamble since changes in the resolving clauses may affect the preamble.

THE COURTESY RESOLUTION:

A committee is often charged with the duty of drafting and presenting to the assembly a courtesy resolution.

Ordinarily courtesy resolutions express appreciation of a convention to those who arranged accommodations for the physical needs or rendered it service. No opposing vote is taken on a courtesy resolution.

705   **SUBSIDIARY MOTIONS**

Subsidiary motions assist in treating or disposing of the main motion and, sometimes other motions. Subsidiary motions arise out of consideration of another motion and are used to modify, delay action on, or dispose of the pending motion. When a subsidiary motion is stated by the chair, it supersedes a motion of lower rank which was pending and becomes the immediately pending question. Subsidiary motions have a definite order of precedence:

Highest ranking is: Lay on the table

Next highest   Previous question (stop debate and vote
                                  now)
                      Limit or extend debate
                      Postpone definitely
                      Refer to a committee
                      Amend

Lowest ranking is Postpone indefinitely

Certain subsidiary motions may be applied to others such as: amend may be amended, referred to a committee, postponed definitely and limit or extend debate on the amendment.

POSTPONE INDEFINITELY

This is a motion that rejects the main motion, and it cannot be moved if anything is pending except the main motion. It is useful only when the opponents of a measure are in doubt as to whether they control the majority vote.

RULES GOVERNING THE MOTION:

1. Is not in order when another has the floor

2. Requires recognition

3. Requires a second

4. Is debatable — opens the main motion to debate

5. Is not amendable

6. Requires a majority vote

7. Only an affirmative vote may be reconsidered

THE FORM IS: "I move that the question be postponed indefinitely."

"I move that the motion . . . . . be postponed indefinitely."

AMEND

This motion is made to change the wording of the main motion before final action is taken upon it.

RULES GOVERNING THE MOTION:

1. Is not in order when another has the floor

2. Requires recognition

3. Requires a second

4. Is debatable when applied to a debatable motion

5. Is amendable — (a primary amendment is amendable but a secondary amendment is not amendable)

6. It yields to higher ranking subsidiary motions, all privileged and applicable incidental motions, except "divide" and "consider seriatim".

7. Requires a majority vote even if the motion to be amended requires a higher vote.

8. May be reconsidered

KINDS OF AMENDMENTS:

1. A primary amendment (first degree) amends the pending question and must be germane to it.

2. A secondary amendment (second degree) amends the primary amendment and must be germane to it. Secondary amendments do not apply directly to the pending motion (main motion).

3. Only two amendments may be pending at one time — one of each kind. After either has been disposed of, another amendment may be offered if germane.

4. All debate must be germane to the immediately pending question whether that be a secondary or a primary amendment.

5. Two votes are necessary when dealing with a primary amendment. The first vote is on the amendment. Then the second vote is on the pending main motion as amended or not amended.

6. Three votes are necessary when dealing with a secondary amendment. The first vote is on the secondary amendment, then the second vote is on the primary amendment as amended or not, then the third vote is on the main motion as amended or not.

METHOD OF AMENDING:

1. By adding at the end.

2. By striking out a word or consecutive words.

3. By inserting a word or consecutive words.

4. By striking out and inserting a word or consecutive words.

5. By substitution (when too many changes are necessary)

RULES FOR THE DIFFERENT FORMS OF AMENDMENT:

1. To insert or add words:

    a. Exact place to be inserted must be specified.

    b. After words have been inserted or added, they may not be changed or struck out, except through a reconsideration of the vote, or through an amendment presenting a new question to:

    > Strike out the entire paragraph into which words were inserted, or

    > Strike out a portion of the paragraph including all or part of words inserted or enough other words to make a different question from the one decided by insertion, or

    > Substitute an entire paragraph for the one into which words were inserted.

    c. If a motion to insert certain words in a particular place is voted down, it is still in order to move to:

    > Insert only a part of the same words or insert all or part of the same words together with some others.

    d.   After a paragraph has been inserted or added it may not be struck out except in connection with other paragraphs.

    e.   If inserting a paragraph is voted down, that rejection does not prevent the introduction of any other motion except one that presents essentially the same question.

2.   To strike out words:

    a.   The place must be specified if not otherwise clear.

    b.   Words to be struck out must be in consecutive order.

    c.   If separate words are to be struck out, a motion should be to strike out the entire clause and insert another wording, or present a separate motion for each striking out.

    d.   Words struck out may not be inserted unless the place or wording is so changed as to make a different question.

    e.   If a motion to strike out fails, it is still in order to:

          Strike out only a part of the same words.

          Strike out all or part of the same words along with other words.

    f.   The motion to strike out certain words may be amended only by a secondary amendment to strike out words from the primary amendment. The effect would be to keep the words in the main motion whether or not the primary amendment is adopted.

3.   To strike out and insert words:

    a.   The word "substitute" should not be used for this.

b. There are two types of "strike out and insert"

    a. Certain wording is struck out of one place and different wording is inserted in that same place.

    b. Certain wording is struck out of one place and inserted in a different place.

c. After the matter has been inserted it may not be struck out. Except by reconsideration of the vote taken on it.

d. If the motion to strike out and insert is voted down, it is still in order to make either of the parts of a separate motion with the same words, or make another motion to strike out and insert with words materially different.

4. To substitute

The motion to substitute often provides a convenient and timesaving method for handling a poorly framed main motion or resolution. A motion to strike out an entire paragraph, article or a complete main motion or resolution is called a motion to substitute. The motion to substitute is a primary amendment and can be moved only when no other amendment is pending.

COMMIT OR REFER

This motion is a motion to refer a pending question to one or more persons.

RULES GOVERNING THE MOTION:

1. Is not in order when another has the floor

2. Requires recognition

3. Requires a second

4. Is debatable as to the desirability of committing and to appropriate details of the motion to commit.

5. Is amendable as to the committees composition, manner of composition, instructions to the committee.

6. Requires a majority vote

7. Can be reconsidered if the committee has not begun consideration of the question.

This motion may be applied to a main motion or to a main motion with adhering amendments. Variations of the motion are:

Committee of the whole

quasi committee of the whole

informal consideration.

Details to be covered in the motion are: the kind of committee to which the question is to be referred such as, a standing committee, a special committee. If the motion is to be referred to a special committee, include the number to be on the committee and the method of selection, unless provided in the bylaws. Instructions should include what it is to do and when it is to report and if the committee has power to act.

FORM OF THE MOTION

"I move to refer the question to a committee."

"I move to refer the question to the (name the standing committee)."

"I move to recommit the motion to (name the committee)."

"I move to refer the motion to a committee of three appointed by the chair."

"I move to refer the question to the executive committee with full power."

"I move that we consider the question informally."

POSTPONE DEFINITELY (TO A CERTAIN TIME)

This is the motion by which action on a pending question can be put off, within limits, to a definite day, meeting, or hour or until a certain event.

RULES GOVERNING THE MOTION:

1. Is not in order when another has the floor

2. Requires recognition

3. Requires a second

4. Is debatable only as to propriety and details of postponement.

5. Is amendable only as to time to which the question is to be postponed

6. Requires a majority vote in its simple and usual form.

7. Requires a 2/3 vote if made a special order or the special order.

8. Can be reconsidered.

FORM OF THE MOTION:

"I move to postpone consideration of the question until three PM."

"I move to postpone consideration of the question until after lunch."

"I move to postpone consideration of this question until our next session."

"I move to postpone consideration of this question until our next session and that it be made a special order for two PM."

"I move that the question be postponed to the next regular meeting and that it be made the special order for that day."

There are limits on postponement. A question can be postponed only until the close of the next session. In convention meetings, a motion may not be postponed beyond the last meeting of the convention.

In a meeting the motion to postpone definitely can be renewed after sufficient progress in business or debate to make it essentially a new question.

LIMIT OR EXTEND DEBATE

This motion is to limit the time that will be devoted to discussion of a pending question or to modify or remove limitations already imposed on its discussion.

RULES GOVERNING THE MOTION:

1. Is not in order when another has the floor

2. Requires recognition

3. Is not debatable

4. Is amendable only as to time

5. Requires a 2/3 vote (because it suspends the rules)

6. Can be reconsidered.

FORM OF THE MOTION:

"I move to limit debate on this question to one hour."

"I move to limit the time of each speaker on the question to three minutes."

"I move that the time of the speaker be extended by ten minutes."

PREVIOUS QUESTION Stop debate and vote now

This motion is to stop debate and take an immediate vote on the pending question or a series of pending questions.

RULES GOVERNING THE MOTION:

1. Is not in order when another has the floor

2. Requires recognition

3. Requires a second

4. Is not debatable

5. Is not amendable

6. Requires a 2/3 vote

7. May be reconsidered only before any vote has been taken under its orders.

Form:

"I move to vote immediately on the motion."

"I move to vote now on all pending questions."

"I move the previous question."

"I move the previous question on all pending questions."

If the previous question is adopted, votes are taken immediately on the question specified. If lost, debate continues on the immediately pending question. This motion does not prevent the making of the motion to "lay on the table" or any privileged motion.

LAY ON THE TABLE Temporarily

This motion puts aside the pending question temporarily when something more urgent arises.

RULES GOVERNING THE MOTION:

1. Is not in order when another has the floor

2. Requires recognition

3. Requires a second

4. Is not debatable, however a member may make a short statement as to the reason for making the motion.

5. Is not amendable — may not be qualified in any way.

6. Requires a majority vote.

7. May not be reconsidered, but may be renewed after progress in debate or taken from the table by majority vote.

FORM:

"I move to lay the question on the table."

"I move that the resolution be layed on the table."

The motion to lay on the table cannot be qualified in any way. To "lay on the table until" is out of order. The motion to use is "postpone definitely".

Members should avoid saying "I move to table" or "that the motion be tabled".

When the motion is laid on the table, all adhering motions go with it. When taken from the table, the motion comes back in the same manner with all adhering motions with it.

The motion may be renewed on the same day if there has been material progress made in business or debate.

If there is no urgency for setting aside the question, the motion "to lay on the table" is dilatory and the chair should rule it out of order.

706 PRIVILEGED MOTIONS

Privileged motions deal with special matters of immediate importance which, without debate, are allowed to interrupt consideration of anything else. They have no bearing on the subject matter before the assembly.

They are the highest ranking motions. They do not relate to the business of the meeting. They do have an order of rank.

Highest ranking is: Fix the time to which to adjourn
Adjourn
Recess
Raise a question of privilege

Lowest ranking: Call for the orders of the day

All except "Call for the orders of the day" may be incidental main motions if introduced while no business is pending.

CALL FOR THE ORDERS OF THE DAY

This motion requires that the assembly conform to its agenda, program, or order of business, or to take up a general or special order due to come up.

RULES GOVERNING THE MOTION:

1. Is in order when another has the floor

2. Does not require recognition

3. Does not require a second

4. Is not debatable

5. Is not amendable

6. Upon the call by a single member the orders of the day must be enforced, unless set aside by a 2/3 vote

7. Cannot be reconsidered.

FORM:

"I call for the orders of the day."

QUESTION OF PRIVILEGE

This motion is to enable a member to secure immediate decision and action by the presiding officer on a request that concern the comfort, convenience, rights or privileges of the assembly or of himself as a member, or permission to present a motion of urgent nature, even though other business is pending.

RULES GOVERNING THE MOTION

1. Can interrupt a speaker if it requires immediate decision or action.

2. Does not require recognition.

3. Is not debatable.

4. Is not amendable.

5. Requires no vote.

6. Chair rules — subject to appeal.

7. Chair's ruling may not be reconsidered.

8. Can have no motion applied to it except "withdraw".

FORM:

Member: "I rise to a question of privilege of the assembly."

Chair: "State your question of privilege."

Member: "May we have the door closed. We cannot hear the speaker because of the noise."

Chair: "Your request is granted."

Member: "I rise to a question of personal privilege."

Chair: "State your privilege."

Member: "May I be excused from further attending the session, I have a committee meeting to attend."

Chair: "Your privilege is granted."

RECESS

Recess is a short intermission in the assembly's proceedings which does not close the meeting and after which business will be immediately resumed at exact point where it was interrupted.

RULES GOVERNING THE MOTION:

1. Is not in order when another has the floor.

2. Requires recognition.

3. Requires a second.

4. Is not debatable.

5. Is amendable as to the length of the recess.

6. Requires a majority vote.

7. May be reconsidered.

FORM:

"I move that we recess for ten minutes."

"I move to recess until 2:00 p.m."

When a motion to recess is made when no business is pending it is a main motion. When a recess is provided for in the adopted program, the chair, without further action by the assembly announces the fact and declares the assembly in recess when the specified time arrives. If the chair fails to announce the recess a member may call for the orders of the day.

ADJOURN

This motion is to terminate a meeting.

RULES GOVERNING THE MOTION:

1. Cannot interrupt a speaker

2. Requires recognition

3. Is not debatable

4. Is not amendable

5. Requires a majority vote

6. May not be reconsidered

7. Can have no motion applied to it except "withdraw"

FORM:

"I move that we adjourn."

"I move to adjourn."

After the motion to adjourn has been moved, the following parliamentary steps are in order while the motion to adjourn is pending; or after the assembly has voted to adjourn:

1. Inform the assembly of business requiring attention before adjournment.

2. Make important announcements.

3. Make (but not to take up) a motion to reconsider a previous vote.

4. Move to reconsider and enter on the minutes.

5. Give notice of a motion to be made at the next meeting (or on the next day in a session consisting of daily meetings) where the motion requires previous notice, or

6. Move to set a time for an adjourned meeting if the time for the next meeting is not already settled.

No meeting is closed until the chair has declared that the meeting "is adjourned" (or stands adjourned). The members should not leave their seats until such time as the declaration is made.

A meeting can be adjourned without a motion if the hour for adjournment has been prescheduled. The chair simply announces the fact and declares the meeting adjourned. Also, when it appears there is no further business, the agenda having been completed, the chair may say, "Is there any further business?" If no response — "Since there is no further business, the meeting is adjourned."

FIX THE TIME TO WHICH TO ADJOURN

This motion provides for a continuation of business at another meeting which is called an adjourned meeting.

RULES GOVERNING THE MOTION:

1. Is not in order when another has the floor

2. Requires recognition

3. Requires a second

4. Is not debatable

5. Is amendable as to date, hour, place

6. Requires a majority vote

7. May be reconsidered

FORM

"I move that when we adjourn we adjourn to meet tomorrow at 2:00 p.m. in the community room."

"I move that when we adjourn we adjourn to meet tomorrow at the same time and place."

Adoption of the motion to fix the time to which to adjourn does not adjourn the present meeting. The date for an adjourned meeting must be set for a time prior to the next regular meeting. The present meeting and the meeting on the date designated are two meetings constituting one session. At the adjourned meeting, except for the reading of the minutes, business will be taken up from the place at which the previous meeting adjourned or at which questions were postponed.

707   **INCIDENTAL MOTIONS**

Incidental motions apply to the method of transacting business rather than to the business itself. They relate in different ways to the pending business and deal with questions of procedure arising out of another pending motion.

An incidental motion is incidental to other motions or matter out of which it arises and with few exceptions is so related to the main motion that it must be decided immediately before business can proceed. An incidental motion is in order only when legitimately incidental to another pending motion, or when legitimately incidental in some other way to the business at hand. Each incidental motion has its own rules determining conditions under which it is applicable.

POINT OF ORDER

This motion is to call to the attention of the chair a violation of a rule when the chair neglects to do so.

RULES GOVERNING THE MOTION:

1. Is in order when another has the floor — can interrupt a speaker.

2. Does not require recognition.

3. Does not require a second.

4. Is not debatable.

5. Is not amendable.

6. Chair rules. If submitted to the assembly, a majority vote is required.

7. May not be reconsidered.

FORM:

"I rise to a point of order."

"Point of order."

Chair: "State your point."

Member: "The member is not speaking to the motion but to another subject."

Chair: "Will the member please be seated, or speak to the
pending motion."

Member: "Point of order."

Chair: "State your point."

Chair: "The chair rules that the amendment is germane." or
"The chair rules that the amendment is not germane."

The chair may ask the assembly to decide:

Chair: "Those who are of the opinion that the amendment
is germane, say 'Aye'. Those opposed say 'No'. The
noes have it, the amendment is not germane." or
"The ayes have it, the amendment is germane."

A point of order must be raised at the time the breach
occurs. The ruling of the chair may be appealed. If the
point of order is referred to the assembly for decision, the
ruling of the assembly may not be appealed.

APPEAL

The motion allows two members who disagree with the
ruling of the chair to submit it to the assembly for a decision.

RULES GOVERNING THE MOTION:

1. Is in order when another has the floor. Must be proposed
immediately.

2. Does not require recognition.

3. Requires a second.

4. Is debatable, unless it
   a. relates to indecorum or transgression of debate.
   b. relates to priority of business.
   c. is made during a division of the assembly.
   d. is made while the immediately pending question is
   undebatable.

5. Is not amendable.

6. Requires a majority vote in the negative to overrule the chair's decision.

7. A majority vote or tie vote sustains the decision of the chair.

8. Takes precedence over any question and must be decided immediately.

FORM:

Member: "I appeal from the decision of the chair."

Another member: "Second the motion."

Chair: "There has been an appeal from the decision of the chair." (At this point the chair gives reasons for the decision. Members may speak only once to the question. The chair may speak a second time at the close of the debate.)

Chair: "Shall the decision of the chair be sustained? Those in favor of sustaining the chair say 'Aye'. Those opposed say 'No'." "The 'Ayes' have it and the decision of the chair is sustained." or "The noes have it and the decision of the chair is reversed."

The presiding officer does not leave the chair but debates while in the chair. Appeals may be applied only to rulings of the chair, not to the opinion of the chair.

SUSPEND THE RULES

This motion is used when the assembly wishes to do something that cannot be done without violating its own rules, but which does not conflict with the constitution, bylaws, local, state, or national law, or with the fundamental rules of parliamentary procedure.

RULES GOVERNING THE MOTION:

1. Is not in order when another has the floor.

2. Requires recognition.

3. Requires a second.

4. Is not debatable.

5. Is not amendable.

6. Requires a two-thirds vote.

7. Can have no motion applied to it except "withdraw."

8. Must be decided immediately.

FORM

"I move to suspend rule #5."

"I move to suspend the rule which interferes with . . . . "

Rules that may not be suspended:

1. Rules contained in bylaws, constitution unless the particular specified provided for its own suspension.

2. Rules protecting absentees or a basic right of the individual member.

Rules that may be suspended:

1. Rules of order (parliamentary procedure) by a 2/3 vote.

2. Standing rules (rules that do not relate to parliamentary procedure, such as hours for beginning and ending meetings.

The motion may be renewed only by unanimous consent for the same purpose at the same meeting. It may be renewed for the same purpose after and adjournment even if the meeting is held on the same day. Any number of motions to suspend the rules for different purposes can be offered in the same meeting.

OBJECT TO THE CONSIDERATION OF A QUESTION

This motion is used to avoid a particular embarrassing or undesirable original main motion from being discussed.

RULES GOVERNING THE MOTION:

1. Can interrupt proceedings. Must be made before there is any debate or subsidiary motion stated by the chair.

2. Does not require a second.

3. Is not debatable.

4. Is not amendable.

5. A two-thirds vote against consideration required to sustain the objection.

6. Negative vote sustaining the objection may be reconsidered.

FORM

"I object to the consideration of the question (resolution)."

If an objection to the consideration is sustained, and the main motion is dismissed for that session it cannot be renewed except by unanimous consent or by reconsideration of the vote on the objection. The presiding officer may initiate an objection to the consideration just as he can raise a point of order on his own.

DIVISION OF A QUESTION

A main motion, or an amendment to it, consisting of two or more parts capable of standing alone, may be divided into two or more questions by the adoption of this motion.

RULES GOVERNING THE MOTION:

1. Is not in order when another has the floor.

2. Requires recognition.

3. Requires a second.

4. Is not debatable.

5. Is amendable.

6. Requires a majority vote.

7. Cannot be reconsidered.

FORM

"I move to divide the motion so as to consider separately the
.... and the ...."

The motion to divide must clearly state the manner in which the question is to be divided. A motion cannot be divided unless each part presents a proper question for the assembly to act on if none of the other part is adopted. A resolution cannot be divided if it contains several propositions which would be impossible to separate without rewriting it.

DIVISION OF THE ASSEMBLY

This motion is used when a member doubts the result of a vote announced by the chair.

RULES GOVERNING THE MOTION:

1. Is in order when another has the floor and at any time after the question has been put, even after the vote has been announced.

2. Does not require recognition.

3. Is not debatable.

4. Is not amendable.

5. Does not require a vote, since a single member can demand a division.

6. Cannot be reconsidered.

FORM:

"I call for a division."

"Division."

A division must be called for prior to the stating of another motion. If a member desires the vote to be counted he must make a motion to that effect, which requires a second and a majority vote.

CONSIDER BY PARAGRAPH OR SERIATIM

This motion provides for long motions or reports consisting of several paragraphs, resolutions, or sections to be considered by opening different parts to debate and amendment separately without a division of the question.

RULES GOVERNING THE MOTION:

1. Is not in order when another has the floor.

2. Requires recognition.

3. Is not debatable.

4. Is amendable.

5. Requires a majority vote.

6. Cannot be reconsidered.

FORM:

"I move that the resolution be considered by paragraph."

Each paragraph is open to debate and amendment if the consideration by paragraph is adopted. When no further amendments are proposed and debate ceases on the paragraph, the chair proceeds to the next until all have been opened to debate and amendment. After all paragraphs are amended the entire series is open to further amendment and debate. At this time additional parts may be inserted or parts may be struck out. A single vote is taken on the adoption of the entire series.

WITHDRAW A MOTION

This motion enables a member who proposed a motion to remove it from consideration by the assembly.

RULES GOVERNING THE MOTION:

1. Cannot interrupt a speaker.

2. Requires recognition.

3. Requires no second as it is a request.

4. Is not debatable.

5. Is not amendable.

6. Requires no vote.

7. Applies to all motions.

FORM:

"I withdraw my motion."

The consent of the seconder is not necessary. A motion can be withdrawn if there is no objection or with permission from the assembly up to the moment the final vote is taken.

MOTIONS RELATING TO METHODS OF VOTING AND THE POLLS

Motions that provide for different ways of obtaining a vote or for the opening and closing of the polls.

RULES GOVERNING THE MOTION:

1. Not in order when another has the floor.

2. Require recognition.

3. Require a second.

4. Are not debatable.

5. Are not amendable.

6. Require a majority vote except a motion to close the polls.

   A 2/3 vote is required to close the polls.

   A majority vote to reopen the polls.

FORMS:

"I move that when the vote is taken on the pending question that it be taken by ballot."

"I move that the polls be closed."

"I move to reopen the polls for ten minutes."

MOTIONS RELATING TO NOMINATIONS

Motions that allow members to specify method of nominating and the closing and reopening of nominations if it is not prescribed in the bylaws or the rules of order.

RULES GOVERNING THE MOTION:

1. Are not in order when another has the floor.

2. Requires recognition.

3. Require a second.

4. Are not debatable.

5. Are not amendable.

6. Requires a majority vote, except to close nominations which requires a 2/3 vote.

7. May be reconsidered, except the motion to close nominations or an affirmative vote on a motion to reopen nominations.

FORM:

"I move that nominations be made from the floor."

"I move that nominations be made by ballot."

"I move that nominations be made by a committee of three appointed by the chair."

"I move that nominations be closed."

"I move that nominations be reopened for the office of treasurer."

MOTIONS THAT ARE REQUESTS

In a business meeting a member may wish to obtain information or to have something done that requires permission from the assembly. Requests grow out of business of the assembly are:

Points of information

Parliamentary inquiry

Read a paper

To be excused from duty

Any other privilege

RULES GOVERNING THESE MOTIONS:

1. Are in order when another has the floor.

2. Do not require a second.

3. Are not debatable.

4. Are not amendable.

5. No vote is taken.

FORM:

"I rise for a point of information."

"I rise to a parliamentary inquiry."

"I ask permission to read a statement."

"I request to be excused from duty."

708 SPECIFIC MAIN MOTIONS THAT HAVE NO RELATION TO THE ORDER OF THE PRECEDENCE OF MOTIONS

These motions are placed in this classification because they serve a function which is described by their name.

They are restoratory motions and are unclassified. They are:

Reconsider

Rescind — Amend something previously adopted

Ratify

Take from the table

Discharge a committee

RECONSIDER

The purpose of reconsidering a vote is to permit correction of hasty, ill-advised, or erroneous action; or to take into account added information or a changed situation that has developed since the taking of the vote.

RULES GOVERNING THE MOTION:

1. Must be made by the one who voted on the prevailing side. Must be made only on the same day, or the next calendar day after the original vote was taken.

2. Is in order when another has the floor assigned, if that member has not yet begun to speak.

3. Does not require recognition, but may not interrupt a speaker.

4. Requires a second.

5. Is debatable when the motion proposed to be reconsidered is debatable. When debatable, opens to debate merits of the motion proposed for reconsideration.

6. Is not amendable.

7. Requires only a majority vote.

8. Cannot be reconsidered.

FORM:

"I move to reconsider the vote on the motion relating to . . . . I voted (for or against) the motion."

RESCIND — AMEND SOMETHING PREVIOUSLY ADOPTED

This is a motion by which an action previously ordered or taken can be changed, repealed or annulled.

RULES GOVERNING THE MOTION:

1. Is not in order when another has the floor.

2. Requires recognition.

3. Requires a second.

4. Is debatable; debate may go into the merits of the motion which it is proposed to rescind.

5. Is amendable.

6. Requires a 2/3 vote or a vote of a majority of the entire membership except when notice has been given at a previous meeting; then the motion requires a majority vote.

7. Only the negative vote may be reconsidered.

FORM:

"I move to rescind the motion relating to. . . . adopted at the June meeting . . . . I gave previous notice at the previous meeting."

"I move to rescind the resolution which authorized . . . ..
Previous notice was given at the last meeting."

"I move to amend the motion by striking out . . . Previous
notice was given at the last meeting."

"I move to amend the motion adopted at the June meeting
by inserting . . . . "

RATIFY

To ratify means to approve, confirm, validate, make
legal, etc. The object of the motion to ratify is to approve or
legalize an act.

RULES GOVERNING THE MOTION:

1. Cannot interrupt a speaker.

2. Requires recognition.

3. Requires a second.

4. Is debatable.

5. Is amendable.

6. Majority vote.

7. Can be reconsidered.

FORM:

"I move that we ratify the action taken by the executive
committee."

"I move that we ratify the action taken by . . . . "

TAKE FROM THE TABLE

The motion to take from the table is used when it is desired to bring back the question for further consideration that was laid on the table.

RULES GOVERNING THE MOTION:

1. Is not in order when another has the floor.

2. Requires recognition.

3. Requires a second.

4. Is not debatable.

5. Is not amendable.

6. Requires a majority vote.

7. Cannot be reconsidered.

FORM:

"I move to take from the table the motion relating to . . . ."

DISCHARGE A COMMITTEE

This is a motion by means of which further consideration of a question or subject may be taken away from the committee. The assembly can take the matter out of a committee's hands after referring it to a committee and before the committee has made a final report on it. So long as a question is in the hands of a committee, the assembly cannot consider another motion involving practically the same thing.

RULES GOVERNING THE MOTION:

1. Is not in order when another has the floor.

2. Requires recognition.

3. Requires a second.

4. Is debatable: debate may go into the merits of the question which is in the hands of the committee.

5. Is amendable by the basic processes of amending and may instruct the committee instead of discharging it.

6. Requires a 2/3 vote or a vote of a majority of the entire membership, or only a majority vote if notice has been given at a previous meeting or in the call to the present meeting.

7. Only the negative vote may be reconsidered.

FORM:

"I move that the committee to which was referred the motion regarding . . . . be discharged."

"I move that the committee appointed to investigate the question of . . . . be discharged and that this matter be made a special order for our next meeting."

"I move that the membership committee be discharged from further consideration of the motion referred to it on . . . . "

709 RULES GOVERNING MOTIONS

RANKING MOTIONS

ORDER OF PRECEDENCE

PRIVILEGED MOTIONS	Can Interrupt Speaker	Requires Second	Debatable	Amendable	Vote Required	Can Be Reconsidered
Fix the time TO WHICH to adjourn	no	yes	no	yes	majority	yes
Adjourn (unqualified)	no	yes	no	no	majority	no
Take a Recess	noi	yes	no	yes	majority	no
Question of privilege	yes	no	no	no	•	no
Orders of the Day	yes	no	no	no	•	no
SUBSIDIARY MOTIONS						
Lay on the Table (temporarily)	no	yes	no	no	majority	no
Previous Question (stop debate)	no	yes	no	no	2/3	yes
Limit or Extend Debate	no	yes	no	yes	2/3	yes
Postpone to Certain Time	no	yes	yes	yes	majority	yes
Refer to Committee	no	yes	yes	yes	majority	yes
Amend	no	yes	yes	yes	majority	yes
Postpone Indefinitely	no	yes	yes	no	majority	aff. vote only
MAIN MOTION	no	yes	yes	yes	majority	yes

• Chair usually decides. Majority if put to vote.

MOTIONS THAT BRING A QUESTION AGAIN BEFORE THE ASSEMBLY

SPECIFIC MAIN MOTIONS	Can Interrupt Speaker	Requires Second	Debatable	Amendable	Vote Required	Can Be Reconsidered
Reconsider	no	yes	yes*	no	majority	no
Ratify	no	yes	yes	yes	majority	yes
Rescind	no	yes	yes	yes	(1)	neg. Vote only
Take from the table	no	yes	no	no	majority	no
Discharge Committee	no	yes	yes	yes	2/3	neg. vote only
Amend something previously adopted	no	yes	yes	yes	(1)	neg. vote only

* Except when the motion to be reconsidered is debatable.

(1) Requires a 2/3 vote when applied to a Constitution, bylaws or special rules. A majority vote when notice is given at a previous meeting or a majority vote of the entire membership without notice.

710   INCIDENTAL MOTIONS

Incidental motions are so-called because they are incidental, or arise out of a motion on which they have a bearing. They have no rank among themselves, but depend on the circumstances. These motions, or requests are of such nature that each has to be decided as it arises. They may interrupt business temporarily. They are not debatable, except the motion to "appeal from the decision of the chair". Incidental motions must be decided before the main motion.

NO RANK	Can Interrupt Speaker	Requires Second	Debatable	Amendable	Vote Required	Can Be Reconsidered
Point of Order	yes	no	no	no	•	no
Appeal from the decision of chair	yes	yes	limited	no	majority	yes
Suspend the Rules of Order	no	yes	no	no	2/3	no
Suspend Standing Rules	no	yes	no	no	majority	no
Object to Consideration	yes	no	no	no	2/3	neg. vote only
Division of a Question (motion)	no	yes	no	yes	majority	no
Consider by paragraph (Seriatim)	no	yes	no	yes	majority	no
Division of Assembly (vote)	yes	no	no	no	none	no
Close Polls	no	yes	no	yes	2/3	no
Reopen Polls	no	yes	no	yes	majority	neg. vote only
Close Nominations	no	yes	no	yes	2/3	no
Reopen Nominations	no	yes	no	yes	majority	neg. vote only
Parliamentary Inquiry	yes	no	no	no	none	no
Request for Information	yes	no	no	no	none	no
Excused for Duty	no	yes	yes	yes	majority	neg. vote only
Withdraw a motion	(1)	(2)	no	no	majority	neg. vote only
Create a Blank	no	yes	no	no	majority	no
Fill a Blank	no	no	yes	no	majority	yes
Request to Read a Paper	(1)	(2)	no	no	majority	yes
Motions Relating to Voting	no	yes	no	yes	majority	no

* Chair usually decides. Majority if put to a vote.

(1) If not granted by general consent, can be moved by person requesting permission.

(2) Yes, if motion made by person requesting permission.

8

BYLAWS

801   BYLAW COMMITTEE MEMBERS

The bylaws of a membership organization are those rules adopted by the members to regulate and manage its business and to set forth the rights and duties of its members. They also define the specific duties and responsibilities of directors and elected officers.

Bylaws are prepared by a committee. It is the committee's function to make certain that the bylaw provisions do not conflict with the actual operating procedures and objectives of the organization. The bylaws of membership organizations vary, no two sets of bylaws are exactly the same, the difference being reflected in the objectives of the organization.

802   COMMITTEE ON BYLAWS

A committee to prepare a set of bylaws usually should be large, and include, in addition to the persons interested, all those who are likely to consume much time in discussing the bylaws. By this means the committee members can thoroughly discuss the provisions which usually require hours and probably days. After the large committee has had one or two meetings on the subject and have come to an agreement, it should appoint a sub-committee of two or three to actually write the bylaws. This sub-committee should be careful to see that everything relating to a subject is placed in the same or adjacent article. Each article may have several sub-divisions. There should be nothing in the bylaws that conflict with other articles.

Expressions used in bylaws should be clear. Under the article on 'officers' if the term is simply stated as "one year" at the end of one year the term expires, whether or not a successor has been elected. By using the expression, "or (or and) until the successor is elected" the officer holds over until the successor is elected, in case of a failure to elect a successor at the annual meeting. If "or" is used, the organization has a right to declare an office vacant by the same vote that is required to rescind any action taken. If "and" is used, the organization cannot vacate an office.

The sentence structure in bylaws is not the same as that in writing to explain something. Words must be chosen carefully. Each sentence should be written so as to be impossible to quote out of context. A sentence may end with an 'exception clause', such as "except that . . ." or "Except as provided in Article _____ . . . ." or "Provided that . . . ."

803   **CONTENT OF BYLAWS**

Bylaws provide the legal framework within which the organization functions. They should be custom-made to fit each individual organization. The number of articles will be determined by the size and the activities of the organization.

Bylaws are divided into units called ARTICLES assigned with roman numerals. Each article is subdivided into SECTIONS or paragraphs in which arabic numerals are assigned. The word 'article' should be placed in the center of the page and the sections to the left of the page.

804   **PATTERN FOR BASIC BYLAWS**

ARTICLE I

NAME

(May be omitted, if in Article of Incorporation)

ARTICLE II

OBJECT or PURPOSE

(Concisely expressed in a single sentence or phrase separated by semicolons or in lettered sub paragraphs.)

(May be omitted if in Articles of Incorporation)

ARTICLE III

MEMBERS

1. The method of uniting with the organization should be clearly stated.

2. Qualifications and eligibility.

3. Kinds of membership: Active, Associate, Sustaining, Life Honorary, etc.

4. How admitted.

5. Limitation as to number of members.

6. Rights and duties of each class of membership.

7. How membership is terminated.

8. Reinstatement of member.

9. Anything else pertaining to members.

ARTICLE IV

FINANCES

1. Required dues — fees.

2. Date when payable, whether annually, quarterly, etc.

3. Time and procedure for notifying members if they become delinquent in payment.

4. Penalties for non-payment of dues.

5. Date when member will be dropped for non-payment of dues.

6. Fiscal year.

7. Anything else pertaining to finances.

ARTICLE V

DISSOLUTION

(Should this organization become dissolved, the Executive Board shall determine distributions of net assets to such organizations whose purposes qualify them for tax exemption under Federal regulations, and whose endeavors are in accord with the stated objectives of this organization.) (Or such wording as the organization may determine.)

ARTICLE VI

OFFICERS

1. Great care should be taken in writing this article.

2. Number of officers, titles and qualifications.

3. Term of office, powers and duties.

4. Manner of election — Method of nominating.

5. Vacancies — how filled.

6. Removal from office.

7. Appointed officers.

8. (Directors — how elected — how many).

ARTICLE VII

MEETINGS

1. Kinds of meetings; such as Board, Regular, Special, Annual.

2. When held.

3. Quorum.

ARTICLE VIII

CONVENTIONS or CONSTITUENT DIVISIONS

ARTICLE IX

EXECUTIVE BOARD or BOARD OF DIRECTORS

1. Composition of Board.

2. Powers.

3. When and how often to meet.

4. Quorum.

ARTICLE X

COMMITTEES

1. Standing committees — listed by name.

2. Composition of standing committee, manner of election or appointment, duties.

3. (Shall president be ex officio except nominating committee).

4. Time of meetings.

ARTICLE XI

PARLIAMENTARY AUTHORITY

This adopted authority furnishes the rules which guide on all matters not covered by its Charter, Bylaws, Standing Rules.

ARTICLE XII

AMENDMENTS TO BYLAWS

1. Specify the procedure, the notice, the vote, etc.

2. The wording of this article should avoid redundant phraseology such as amend, alter, add to, or repeal, amend in any other way. The word amend covers any change, whether a word or paragraph to be struck out.

****

Additional articles may be added or placed before the article on parliamentary authority. Some large organizations have 'departments' which should follow the article on committees. Some organizations have an article on 'disciplinary procedures'.

IMPORTANCE OF BYLAWS

Bylaws have a direct bearing on the rights of members within the organization — whether they are present or absent from the meeting. Every member should be given a copy of the bylaws and every member should be familiar with them. When a member joins an organization that member agrees to abide by its bylaws.

805   PRESENTING THE BYLAWS

After the proposed bylaws have been thoroughly examined by the full committee to be sure there are no inconsistencies or ambiguities, they should be typed and circulated to the membership well in advance of the meeting in which they are to be voted on. Copies should be shown to the parliamentarian and other legal advisors so that any legal or technical question can be resolved ahead of time. Advance circulation also enables the members to vote more intelligently on them.

When the chair calls on the bylaw committee to report, the reporting member says, 'By direction of the committee, I move the adoption of the proposed bylaws." No second is necessary as it comes from a committee.

Chair: "The question is on the adoption of the bylaws. The reporting member will now read the proposed bylaws, one article or one section at a time. After each article or section is read, it will be open to debate and amendment. When amendment of one article or section is complete, the next one will be considered. No section or article will be adopted until all have been opened to amendment."

With this explanation from the chair, the members may discuss or amend each provision. After the last section or article has been completed the chair says, "Are there any further amendments to any section or article?" If there are further amendments they are considered. When there are no further amendments the chair says, "The question is on the adoption of the bylaws as amended. Those in favor will please rise." Thank you. "Those opposed please rise. There being two-thirds in the affirmative, the bylaws are adopted. If bylaws are being adopted for the first time, only a majority vote is necessary, which may be taken by voice.

806   AMENDMENTS TO BYLAWS

After bylaws have served for a period of time it may be necessary to amend portions of them. The motion to amend the bylaws is an incidental main motion, and subject to the same rules as a main motion, except that the vote required for its adoption is specified in the bylaws. Since the proposed amendment is a main motion, it may be amended which required no previous notice and only a majority vote even though the proposed amendment to the bylaws requires previous notice and a higher vote. The proposed amendment, however, must be germane to which it applies.

Some organizations provide that the proposed amendment be given to the bylaw committee who studies it and reports the recommendation of the committee to the voting body. A proposed amendment should be stated in language that, if adopted, it may be incorporated directly into the bylaws.

When reporting the amendment or a revision, the committee should fully explain every section, and explain the changes that will result from the proposed change. The organization should know not only the words of the proposed amendments, but also what changes from their former customs will result if the amendments or revision are adopted.

807　　　POINTS TO REMEMBER

No amendment is in order that increases the modification of the article or rule to be amended.

Amendments to strike out a sentence or paragraph, or section deserve special care. In such cases, the existing bylaw is not itself open to consideration, but only the amendment.

An amendment to the bylaws goes into effect immediately with the announcement of the vote adopting it, unless the motion to adopt provides that it become effective at a later time.

If it becomes necessary to change the quorum provision in the bylaws, care should be taken, because, if the rule is struck out first, the quorum will instantly become a majority of the entire membership. The proper procedure is to strike out and insert the new provision in one sentence and vote on it as one question.

An amendment, or a motion to change the numbering of sections paragraphs, etc. is not necessary. It is the duty of the secretary to make such corrections where they become necessary.

The power to amend the bylaws lies primarily with the membership as a whole, but this power may be delegated to the board of directors, unless prohibited by the bylaws or the articles of incorporation.

The procedure for amending the bylaws should be set forth in the bylaws. Any legal requirement, such as the giving of advance notice of the proposed change to the membership must be strictly complied with.

808 **FORM FOR AMENDMENTS
TO THE BYLAWS**

Present Bylaw Article_____   Proposed Amendment to
Section _____   Article_____ Section _____

_____   _____

_____   _____

_____   _____

                              Reason given by proposer __

                              _____

                              _____

                              Advantages _____

                              _____

                              _____

                              Disadvantages _____

                              _____

                              _____

809   FORM FOR PROPOSING A RESOLUTION

WHEREAS, The (Give concise statement of background, purpose, unusual importance, which provides little-known information without which the merits of the resolution would be poorly understood); and

WHEREAS: (After the comma, the next word begins with a capital letter) (Give arguments for the proposed resolution in logical sequence. Each argument should be a separate WHEREAS.); therefore be it

RESOLVED, That . . . .(State action to be taken.).

A resolution may consist of more than one resolving clause.

Note: Each paragraph should close with a semicolon followed by the word "and". The last RESOLVE ends with a period.

810   REVISING BYLAWS

When changes in the bylaws are extensive and scattered throughout the bylaws, a substitution should be made of an entirely new set of bylaws. Amending bylaws by substitution is called a "revision."

When extensive changes are required, the best method is to select a special committee for this purpose, or the bylaw committee may submit a revision.

A copy of the proposed revision with the date it will be considered and voted upon should be sent to each member in advance of the meeting. A revision proposed is a new set of bylaws. It is considered and voted upon under the same procedure as those followed for adopting of the original bylaws. The original bylaws are still in effect and are not before the assembly for consideration.

A revised set of bylaws automatically become effective immediately after the vote adopting the new revision. However, it is possible to adopt a motion to provide that certain portions of them should not become effective until a specified time.

811   PROCEDURE IN HANDLING A REVISION

The presiding officer recognizes the member reporting on the revision. The reporting member says, "At the direction of the committee, I move the adoption of the revised set of bylaws as a substitute for the current bylaws." No second is necessary. The chair indicates that the bylaws will be considered article by article, or, if an article is long and has many sections, it would be considered section by section. The reporting officer then reads the first article. Usually, it is not necessary for the chair to repeat the reading before asking for discussion since everyone should have a copy of the proposed revision. Each article is discussed and any amendments are acted upon at the time. Each amendment requires a majority vote. After all articles have been presented, discussed, amended, the chair asks if there are any further amendments to any article. When there is no further amendments nor any further discussion, a counted standing vote is taken.

812   STANDING RULES

Standing rules usually relate to the details of the administration. Any adopted main motion which has continuing effect is a standing rule. Example: "I move that the secretary send birthday cards to the members." If the motion is adopted it becomes a standing rule and continues in force until it is rescinded. Other examples of standing rules are: Time for the meeting to begin; Location of the meeting; Policy concerning guests; Responsibilities for refreshments; etc. Standing rules are adopted as the need arises at any business meeting without previous notice.

Standing rules for a convention are not the same as the standing rules for the organization. A committee generally prepares the proposed rules which cover such subjects as: seating of the delegates and alternates, length of speeches, privileges of nonvoting members, etc. While these rules apply only to a certain convention, they may be held over from one convention to another convention with only slight changes.

The report of the rules committee follows the report of the credentials committee. These rules may be debated or amended. A single member may demand a separate vote on any individual rule. Usually the rules are adopted as a whole by a two-thirds vote. During the convention any standing rule can be suspended for a specified purpose by a majority vote.